CANADA

travel guide

CANADA
TRAVEL GUIDE 2025

Explore Stunning Natural Wonders and Savor Culinary Delights with Full-Color Maps.

TONY MARK

COPYRIGHT

iii

Table of contents

Canada

SCAN THE QR CODE

- Open your device's camera app
- Point the camera at the QR code
- Ensure the QR code is within the frame and well-lit
- Wait for your device to recognize the QR code
- Once recognized, tap on the map and input for current location for direction and distance to the destination

There's an entire section filled with interactive maps

Quebec City

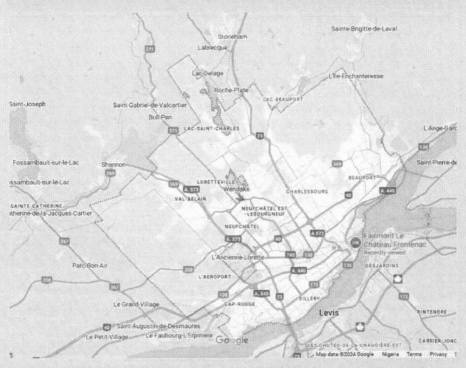

SCAN THE QR CODE

- Open your device's camera app
- Point the camera at the QR code
- Ensure the QR code is within the frame and well-lit
- Wait for your device to recognize the QR code
- Once recognized, tap on the map and input for current location for direction and distance to the destination

There's an entire section filled with interactive maps

Downtown Vancouver

SCAN THE QR CODE

- Open your device's camera app
- Point the camera at the QR code
- Ensure the QR code is within the frame and well-lit
- Wait for your device to recognize the QR code
- Once recognized, tap on the map and input for current location for direction and distance to the destination

There's an entire section filled with interactive maps

INTRODUCTION

Did you know that Canada has the longest coastline in the world? Stretching over 202,080 kilometers, it touches three oceans: the Atlantic, the Pacific, and the Arctic.

A Love Letter to the Great White North

My heart overflows with love for Canada, a land that has captured my soul with its breathtaking beauty, vibrant culture, and warm hospitality.

From the majestic peaks of the Canadian Rockies to the turquoise waters of the Pacific Coast, Canada's landscapes never cease to amaze me. ■ I've wandered through the emerald forests of British Columbia, where sunlight filters through the leaves, casting dappled shadows on the forest floor. ▲ I've kayaked through the calm waters of the Thousand Islands, marveling at the granite giants that rise from the water like silent sentinels. ▬ I've stood in awe at the foot of Niagara Falls, feeling the spray of the mist on my face and the thundering roar of the water in my ears. ✿

But Canada's beauty goes beyond its natural wonders. Its cities, from the cosmopolitan Toronto to the historic Québec City, exude a unique charm that draws you in and makes you feel like home. ■ I've strolled through the cobbled streets of Old Montréal, admiring the French colonial architecture and savoring the aroma of freshly baked croissants. ◗ I've wandered through the bustling markets of Toronto, where vendors from all over the world offer their wares, creating a kaleidoscope of sights, sounds, and smells. ●

And then there are the people, the heart and soul of Canada. Canadians are known for their kindness, generosity, and welcoming spirit. I've been greeted with warm smiles and friendly conversations wherever I've gone. ■ I've shared laughter and stories with locals over cups of hot coffee, feeling a sense of connection that transcends language and culture. ●

Canada is a land of endless possibilities, a place where you can find adventure, relaxation, and everything in between. Whether you're seeking to hike through pristine wilderness, explore vibrant cities, or simply soak up the beauty of nature, Canada has something for everyone. ▲

So, if you're looking for a travel destination that will leave you breathless, fill your heart with joy, and create memories that will last a lifetime, look no further than Canada. This is a land that will steal your heart and leave you longing to return, again and again. ✈

Here are some of the reasons why I love Canada:

- The breathtaking scenery: From the majestic mountains to the sparkling lakes, Canada's natural beauty is simply stunning. ■
- The vibrant culture: Canada is a multicultural country with a rich history and diverse traditions. ●
- The friendly people: Canadians are known for their kindness, generosity, and welcoming spirit. ■
- The endless possibilities: Canada offers a wide variety of activities and experiences for all types of travelers. ▲
- The sense of peace and tranquility: Canada is a vast and uncrowded country, where you can find peace and quiet amidst the beauty of nature. ♟

If you're planning a trip to Canada, here are some tips:

- Do your research: Canada is a large country with diverse regions, so it's important to do your research and decide what you want to see and do before you go. ▄▄
- Book your flights and accommodations in advance: Canada is a popular tourist destination, so it's important to book your flights and accommodations in advance, especially during peak season. ✈▐
- Get a travel visa if you need one: If you're not a citizen of Canada or the United States, you may need to get a travel visa before you go. ▐
- Pack for all types of weather: Canada has a wide variety of climates, so it's important to pack for all types of weather. ▲
- Learn some basic French: While English is spoken widely in Canada, learning some basic French will help you communicate with locals and enhance your experience. ▄▄
- Be respectful of the environment: Canada is a beautiful country, so it's important to be respectful of the environment and leave no trace. ●

I hope this love letter has inspired you to visit Canada. It's a truly magical place that will leave you with memories that will last a lifetime. ✈

Planning Your Canadian Adventure

Grab your toque (that's a beanie for you non-Canadians ●) and let's get this show on the road! Planning a trip to the Great White North might seem like scaling a mountain, but with a little know-how and this guide by your side, you'll be navigating those trails like a seasoned pro in no time. ▲◐

First things first: When to Go? ▇

Canada's a land of dramatic seasons, each with its own unique charm. ❄✳ ✿

- Summer (June-August): Think long sunny days, perfect for hiking, camping, and hitting the beach.   It's peak season, so expect crowds and higher prices.
- Fall (September-November): Oh, the colours! ✿ Imagine forests ablaze with fiery reds, oranges, and yellows. It's a magical time for road trips and cozy cabin getaways. ◐◖
- Winter (December-February): Embrace the snowy wonderland! ❄ Skiing, snowboarding, ice skating, and cozying up by the fire are the name of the game. ▲ Hot tip: pack your warmest layers! ●
- Spring (March-May): Witness nature awaken! ✿ Flowers bloom, wildlife emerges, and the days get longer. It's a great time for exploring cities and enjoying milder weather. ❧

Visa Requirements: ▇

- Nobody wants their adventure to end before it begins. Make sure you have the necessary documentation to enter Canada. Most visitors need an Electronic Travel Authorization (eTA), which you can apply for online. It's quick, easy, and way less stressful than being turned away at the airport! ✈

Packing Essentials: 🎒

Canada's vast and diverse, so pack for all types of weather. Layers are your best friend! Here are some must-haves:

- Comfortable walking shoes: You'll be exploring a lot! 👞
- Waterproof jacket and pants: Because, well, Canada. 🧥
- Warm layers: Even in summer, evenings can get cool. 🧣
- Sunscreen and hat: Protect yourself from those strong Canadian rays. ⬤
- Insect repellent: Mosquitos can be pesky, especially in the wilderness. 🦟
- Adapter: Canada uses 120V electricity and Type A and B plugs. 🔌

Getting Around: 🚗✈️🚆

- Air travel: Domestic flights are a great way to cover long distances. ✈️
- Train travel: VIA Rail offers scenic routes across the country. 🚆 Relax and enjoy the views! ■
- Car rentals: Perfect for exploring at your own pace. 🚗 Just remember, Canada is HUGE! Be prepared for some long drives. ■
- Public transportation: Cities have efficient bus and subway systems. 🚌 ⬤

Money Matters: 💰

Canada uses the Canadian dollar (CAD). ■ Credit cards are widely accepted, but it's always a good idea to have some cash on hand, especially in smaller towns.

Accommodation: 🏠

From cozy cabins to luxurious hotels, Canada has accommodation options to suit every budget and taste. ■⛺ Book in advance, especially during peak season.

Staying Connected: ■■

- Wi-Fi: Available in most hotels and cafes. ▄
- SIM cards: Consider getting a local SIM card for convenient data access. ▌
- Portable charger: Essential for those long days of exploring. ▌

Language: 👤

English is the official language, but French is widely spoken in Quebec. Learning a few basic French phrases will go a long way!"Bonjour," "merci," and "s'il vous plaît" are a great start. ●

Respecting the Land:

Canada's natural beauty is precious. Do your part to protect it by following Leave No Trace principles. Pack out your trash, stay on marked trails, and respect wildlife. ■▲

Most importantly, be open to new experiences, embrace the unexpected, and have fun! Canada is waiting to welcome you with open arms. ● So, pack your bags, grab your sense of adventure, and get ready for the trip of a lifetime!

Understanding Canada

Canada, eh? It's more than just maple syrup and Mounties, you know! ● This country is a vibrant mosaic of cultures and landscapes, a place where towering mountains meet sparkling coastlines, bustling cities blend with peaceful prairies, and ancient traditions intertwine with modern life. ▮

A Land of Many Faces: 🖐

Canada is HUGE! Like, seriously massive. ● It's the second-largest country in the world, spanning six time zones and boasting an incredible diversity of landscapes. From Coast to Coast to Coast: We've got it all! Rugged mountains in the west, rolling prairies in the centre, dense forests in the east, and the icy Arctic in the north. ❄🌲🏔🐚 Each region has its own unique flavour and personality, waiting to be explored.

A Cultural Kaleidoscope: 🖌

Canada's cultural heritage is woven from the threads of Indigenous peoples, European settlers, and immigrants from all corners of the globe. ● This blend of traditions, languages, and beliefs creates a rich and dynamic society.

- First Nations, Inuit, and Métis: Canada's Indigenous peoples have a deep and profound connection to the land, with cultures that date back thousands of years. Their art, music, storytelling, and traditions are an integral part of Canada's identity. 🪘🎵
- European Heritage: The influence of French and British colonization is evident in Canada's architecture, language, and legal system. Explore historic towns and cities, and you'll feel like you've stepped back in time. 🏰

- Multicultural Mosaic: Canada is a welcoming land for immigrants, and this diversity is celebrated throughout the country. From vibrant festivals to delicious cuisine, you'll experience a world of cultures in one place. 🎉●

Connecting with Nature: 🌿
Canadians have a deep appreciation for the natural world. It's in our blood! Whether it's hiking through pristine forests, paddling on crystal-clear lakes, or simply gazing at the starry sky, we love spending time outdoors. ⛺🛶✨

- National Parks: Canada has an incredible network of national parks, protecting some of the most stunning scenery on the planet. From Banff's turquoise lakes to Gros Morne's dramatic fjords, these parks offer endless opportunities for adventure and exploration. ■
- Wildlife Encounters: Keep your eyes peeled for iconic Canadian creatures like bears, moose, whales, and eagles. 🐻🦌🐋🦅 Respect their space and observe them from a safe distance.

City Life with a Twist: ■
Canada's cities are vibrant hubs of culture, innovation, and entertainment. But they also offer a unique blend of urban excitement and natural beauty.

- Green Spaces: Many cities have extensive park systems, offering a welcome escape from the hustle and bustle. Enjoy a picnic lunch, go for a bike ride, or simply relax and soak up the sunshine. ●🚴
- Festival Fun: Throughout the year, cities come alive with festivals celebrating everything from music and art to food and culture. It's a great way to experience the local vibe and connect with the community. 🎶🎉

Understanding Canada is an ongoing journey, one that will fill you with wonder, excitement, and a deep appreciation for this incredible country. So, open your heart and mind, embrace the diversity, and get ready to experience the magic of Canada! ✨

CHAPTER 1

Maritime Magic & Coastal Charms

Did you know that the Bay of Fundy, shared by New Brunswick and Nova Scotia, has the highest tides in the world? Witness the dramatic rise and fall of the tides, explore the ocean floor at low tide.

Newfoundland & Labrador

This province, the most easterly point in North America, is a place where icebergs drift past your doorstep, whales breach in the harbour, and the music of fiddles fills the air. 🎵🪕

A Warm Welcome Awaits: 👋

From the moment I stepped off the ferry in Port aux Basques, I felt like I was stepping into a different world. A world where time seems to slow down, where laughter echoes through the streets, and where strangers greet you with a smile and a "How's she cuttin'?" (that's Newfoundland for "How are you?"). ●

Chasing Icebergs & Whales:

One of my most unforgettable experiences was witnessing the majestic icebergs that drift down from Greenland each spring. Imagine these colossal giants, sculpted by nature, glistening in the sunlight as they slowly make their way along the coast. I took a boat tour in Twillingate, and it was like sailing through a fairytale! We even saw humpback whales breaching and playing in the water – what a sight!

Coastal Charms & Colourful Towns:

Newfoundland and Labrador's coastline is a masterpiece of nature's artistry. Rugged cliffs plunge into the turquoise sea, while charming fishing villages cling to the rocky shores. St. John's, the capital city, is a vibrant hub with colourful houses, lively pubs, and a rich history. Don't miss Signal Hill, where Guglielmo Marconi received the first transatlantic wireless signal!

Hiking Trails & Hidden Gems:

For those who love the outdoors, Newfoundland and Labrador is a paradise. I hiked the Skerwink Trail, a coastal path with breathtaking views of the ocean and dramatic cliffs. The Gros Morne National Park, a UNESCO World Heritage Site, is another must-visit, with its towering mountains, deep fjords, and unique geological formations.

A Feast for the Senses:

Newfoundland and Labrador's culinary scene is a delicious fusion of fresh seafood, local ingredients, and traditional recipes. I savoured every bite of cod tongues (yes, you read that right!), Jiggs dinner (a hearty Sunday meal), and toutons (fried dough with molasses). And let's not forget a cup of strong, dark tea to warm you up on a chilly day.

Music & Merriment:

Music is the heartbeat of Newfoundland and Labrador. Traditional Irish music fills the pubs and community halls, and you'll often find spontaneous kitchen parties breaking out. I joined in a lively sing-along at a local pub, and it was an experience I'll never forget! Come experience the magic for yourself!

Tips for Exploring Newfoundland & Labrador:

- Embrace the pace of life: Things move a little slower here, and that's part of the charm. Relax, enjoy the scenery, and take your time. ●
- Chat with the locals: Newfoundlanders and Labradorians are some of the friendliest people you'll ever meet. Strike up a conversation and you'll be rewarded with stories, laughter, and maybe even an invitation to a kitchen party! 🏠
- Explore beyond St. John's: While the capital city is a must-visit, don't miss the opportunity to explore the smaller towns and villages along the coast. You'll discover hidden gems and experience the true essence of Newfoundland and Labrador. ◆
- Pack for all types of weather: The weather can be unpredictable, so be prepared for sunshine, rain, and even fog. 🌧️
- Learn some local slang: "What are ye at?" and "Stay where you're to 'til I comes where you're at" are just a couple of the colourful expressions you might hear. ●

Newfoundland and Labrador is a place that will steal your heart with its rugged beauty, warm hospitality, and unique culture.

Newfoundland & Labrador

This province stole my heart with its captivating blend of Celtic spirit, dramatic coastlines, and vibrant culture. Imagine a place where the sounds of fiddles and bagpipes fill the air, where charming fishing villages dot the rugged shores, and where the scent of salty sea air mingles with the aroma of fresh lobster. This is Nova Scotia, a land of captivating beauty and heartwarming hospitality.

A Celtic Soul: ♣

From the moment I set foot on Nova Scotian soil, I felt the strong pulse of Celtic heritage. The province's history is deeply intertwined with Scottish, Irish, and Acadian influences, and this rich tapestry is woven into the fabric of everyday life. I visited the Gaelic College in Cape Breton, where I learned about Gaelic language and culture, and even tried my hand at step dancing (with mixed results, I must admit! ●).

Coastal Wonders: ◖✦

Nova Scotia's coastline is a masterpiece of nature's artistry. Rugged cliffs plunge into the sapphire-blue Atlantic, while sandy beaches stretch for miles.

I explored the iconic Cabot Trail, a scenic highway that winds its way through the Cape Breton Highlands National Park, offering breathtaking views of the ocean and mountains. ⬛ The Bay of Fundy, with its dramatic tides – the highest in the world! – is another must-see. I watched in awe as the water rushed in and out, transforming the landscape before my eyes. ●

Charming Towns & Villages: 🏘️
Nova Scotia is dotted with charming towns and villages, each with its own unique character. I wandered through the colourful streets of Lunenburg, a UNESCO World Heritage Site, admiring the historic architecture and browsing the local shops. In Peggy's Cove, I was mesmerized by the iconic lighthouse perched on the rocky shore, a symbol of Nova Scotia's maritime heritage. ⚓

A Foodie's Paradise: ●
Nova Scotia's culinary scene is a celebration of fresh, local ingredients. Lobster, of course, is a must-try, and I savoured every bite of a delicious lobster roll overlooking the harbour. I also indulged in Digby scallops, fresh oysters, and local blueberries – yum! ●

Music & Festivals: 🎵🎻
Music is the lifeblood of Nova Scotia. From traditional Celtic tunes to contemporary folk music, the province has a vibrant music scene. I attended a lively ceilidh (a traditional Gaelic social gathering with music and dancing) and was swept away by the energy and passion of the musicians. 🎻

Tips for Exploring Nova Scotia:

- Embrace the island life: Nova Scotia is made up of a mainland peninsula and Cape Breton Island. Explore both to experience the full diversity of the province. 🏝️
- Hit the road: A road trip is the best way to experience Nova Scotia's stunning scenery and charming towns. Rent a car and explore at your own pace. 🚗

- Go whale watching: Nova Scotia's waters are home to a variety of whales, including humpbacks, minkes, and even the occasional orca. Take a whale watching tour for an unforgettable experience. 🐋
- Learn some Gaelic phrases: While English is the official language, you'll hear Gaelic spoken in some parts of Cape Breton. Learning a few phrases will enhance your experience and show respect for the local culture. "Ciamar a tha thu?" (How are you?) is a good place to start. ⬤
- Immerse yourself in the music: Attend a ceilidh, visit a pub with live music, or catch a performance at the Celtic Colours International Festival. You'll be tapping your toes in no time! 🎵

Nova Scotia is a land of breathtaking beauty, rich history, and warm hospitality. Come experience the magic for yourself! ✨

Prince Edward Island

This magical island, the smallest province in Canada, is a place where time seems to slow down and the pace of life is as gentle as the ocean breeze.

An Island Steeped in Literary Charm

For many, PEI is synonymous with Anne of Green Gables, the beloved children's novel by Lucy Maud Montgomery. The story of Anne Shirley, an orphaned girl with a fiery spirit and an imagination as vast as the sky, has captured hearts around the world.

Following in Anne's Footsteps

A visit to PEI wouldn't be complete without exploring the places that inspired Montgomery's stories.

- Green Gables Heritage Place: This Parks Canada site in Cavendish is home to the iconic Green Gables farmhouse, the setting for Anne's adventures. Step inside and wander through the rooms, imagining Anne's mischievous escapades.
- Lucy Maud Montgomery Birthplace: Visit the charming house where Montgomery was born and spent her early years. Learn about her life and literary career through exhibits and artifacts.
- Anne of Green Gables Museum: Located in Montgomery's childhood home in New London, this museum offers a deeper look into her life and writing process.
- Cavendish Shore: This scenic stretch of coastline is where Montgomery spent many happy summers. Hike along the sandy beaches, explore the red cliffs, and soak up the beauty of the island.

Beyond the Anne Experience

While Anne of Green Gables is a major draw for visitors, PEI has much more to offer.

- Charlottetown: The capital city is a charming blend of historic architecture, vibrant culture, and delicious seafood. Explore the waterfront, visit the Victoria Park, and catch a performance at the Confederation Centre of the Arts.
- Prince Edward Island National Park: This park encompasses stunning beaches, rolling dunes, and lush forests. Hike, bike, swim, or simply relax and enjoy the natural beauty.
- North Rustico: This picturesque fishing village is home to a working harbour, colorful houses, and art galleries. Take a boat tour, sample the local catch, and soak up the maritime atmosphere.
- Red Sands Shore: This unique beach is known for its dramatic red cliffs and expansive sand dunes. Climb to the top of the cliffs for breathtaking views, or explore the dunes on foot or by ATV.

A Culinary Paradise

PEI is a foodie's paradise, with fresh seafood, delicious lobster rolls, and farm-to-table cuisine. Sample the local oysters, indulge in a traditional lobster dinner, and don't forget to try the famous PEI potatoes.

Warm Hospitality & Unforgettable Memories

No matter what your interests are, you're sure to find something to love on Prince Edward Island. From exploring the literary landmarks to soaking up the natural beauty, this island offers an unforgettable experience. And with its friendly locals and welcoming atmosphere, you'll feel right at home in no time.

Tips for Planning Your PEI Adventure

- The best time to visit PEI is during the summer months (June-August), when the weather is warm and sunny. However, the island is beautiful in all seasons, and you can enjoy fewer crowds and lower prices in the spring and fall.

- Renting a car is the best way to get around the island. This will give you the flexibility to explore at your own pace and discover hidden gems.
- Be sure to book your accommodations in advance, especially during peak season.
- Don't forget to pack your swimsuit, sunscreen, and a hat!
- Relax and enjoy the island pace of life!
- Come experience the magic of Prince Edward Island for yourself!

New Brunswick

This province is a hidden gem, a place where Acadian culture thrives, the Bay of Fundy puts on a show with its dramatic tides, and the natural beauty is simply breathtaking. Imagine exploring charming towns with colourful houses, feasting on fresh seafood, and kayaking alongside whales in the shadow of towering cliffs. ✦

New Brunswick is home to a strong and proud Acadian community, descendants of French settlers who arrived in the 17th century. Their vibrant culture, with its unique language, music, and traditions, is woven into the fabric of the province. I visited the Village Historique Acadien, a living history museum where I stepped back in time and experienced life in an Acadian village. I learned about their history, their resilience, and their joie de vivre (joy of living). ●

The Mighty Bay of Fundy: ●C

The Bay of Fundy is a natural wonder, home to the highest tides in the world! Twice a day, over 100 billion tonnes of water flow in and out of the bay, creating a dramatic spectacle. I witnessed this incredible phenomenon at the Hopewell Rocks, where the tides have sculpted towering sandstone formations that resemble flowerpots. At low tide, I walked on the ocean floor, exploring the sea caves and searching for treasures. At high tide, I kayaked around the "flowerpots," marveling at their size and beauty. ▬

Coastal Adventures: 🚴🏊

New Brunswick's coastline is a paradise for outdoor enthusiasts. I cycled along the Fundy Trail Parkway, a scenic route that winds its way along the Bay of Fundy, offering breathtaking views of the cliffs, beaches, and forests. I also spent a day kayaking in the Kouchibouguac National Park, paddling through tranquil lagoons and spotting seals basking in the sun.

Charming Towns & Cities: 🏘️

New Brunswick is dotted with charming towns and cities, each with its own unique character. I explored the historic streets of Saint John, the oldest incorporated city in Canada, and admired the Victorian architecture and vibrant waterfront. In Fredericton, the capital city, I strolled along the Saint John River, visited the Beaverbrook Art Gallery, and enjoyed the lively atmosphere of the Boyce Farmers Market. 💐

A Feast for the Senses: ⚫

New Brunswick's culinary scene is a delicious blend of Acadian flavours and fresh seafood. I savoured poutine râpée (a traditional Acadian dish made with grated potatoes and pork), fresh lobster rolls, and local oysters. And let's not forget the delicious fiddleheads, a springtime delicacy that tastes like a cross between asparagus and spinach. 🍴

Tips for Exploring New Brunswick:

- Immerse yourself in Acadian culture: Visit the Village Historique Acadien, attend a Tintamarre (a noisy Acadian celebration), and try to learn a few French phrases. "Bonjour!" and "Merci!" are a great start. ⚫
- Experience the Bay of Fundy tides: Plan your visit to the Hopewell Rocks around the tide schedule to see the dramatic difference between high and low tide.
- Explore the great outdoors: Hike, bike, kayak, or camp in one of New Brunswick's many national parks and natural areas. ⛰️
- Discover the charm of the cities: Spend some time in Saint John and Fredericton to experience the history, culture, and vibrant atmosphere of these cities.
- Embrace the friendly spirit: New Brunswickers are known for their warm hospitality. Don't be afraid to strike up a conversation with the locals and learn about their way of life. ⚫

New Brunswick is a land of natural wonders, cultural richness, and warm hospitality. Come experience the magic for yourself! ✨

CHAPTER 2

Québec

The Laurentian Mountains are a four-season playground. From skiing and snowboarding in the winter to hiking and kayaking in the summer, this mountain range offers endless opportunities for outdoor adventure.

Montréal

This city, a vibrant mix of European charm and North American energy, captured my heart from the moment I first set foot on its cobblestone streets. Imagine a place where you can wander through historic neighbourhoods, indulge in delectable French pastries, and dance the night away in a trendy club, all while feeling the pulse of a truly international city.

Montréal is a city of contrasts, where historic architecture meets modern skyscrapers, where French and English mingle effortlessly, and where cobblestone streets lead to bustling underground cities.

I loved exploring the charming streets of Old Montréal (Vieux-Montréal), with its 17th-century buildings, horse-drawn carriages, and the majestic Notre-Dame Basilica, a masterpiece of Gothic Revival architecture. But just a few blocks away, I found myself amidst the sleek skyscrapers and trendy boutiques of downtown, a testament to Montréal's modern spirit.

A Foodie's Paradise: ●
Montréal is a foodie's dream come true! From classic French bistros to trendy fusion restaurants, the city offers a culinary adventure for every taste. I indulged in flaky croissants and pain au chocolat at charming patisseries, savoured poutine (fries, cheese curds, and gravy – a must-try!) at a local diner, and enjoyed a gourmet meal at a Michelin-starred restaurant. And let's not forget the bagels! Montréal bagels are legendary, with their slightly sweet flavour and chewy texture. ●

Cultural Melting Pot: ●
Montréal is a true melting pot of cultures, with a diverse population that reflects its history as a hub for immigration. This diversity is celebrated throughout the city, from vibrant festivals to multicultural neighbourhoods. I wandered through the colourful streets of the Plateau Mont-Royal, a trendy neighbourhood with a bohemian vibe, and explored the Quartier Latin, known for its student population and lively nightlife. 🎵

Festival Fun: 🎊
Montréal is a city that loves to celebrate! Throughout the year, the city hosts a variety of festivals, from the world-renowned Montréal International Jazz Festival to the Just for Laughs comedy festival. I was lucky enough to experience the Montréal en Lumière festival, a winter celebration that transforms the city into a magical wonderland of lights and entertainment. ✦

Tips for Exploring Montréal:

- Embrace the bilingualism: Montréal is a predominantly French-speaking city, but English is widely spoken as well. Don't be afraid to try out your French! "Bonjour!" and "Merci!" will go a long way. ●

- Get lost in the underground city: Montréal has an extensive network of underground tunnels connecting shops, restaurants, and metro stations. It's a great way to escape the winter weather and explore the city. ❄

- Climb Mount Royal: For stunning views of the city, climb to the top of Mount Royal, a hill in the heart of Montréal. You can hike, bike, or take the funicular. 🔺

- Explore the museums: Montréal has a wealth of museums, from the Montréal Museum of Fine Arts to the Pointe-à-Callière, an archaeology and history museum. 🎨

- Enjoy the nightlife: Montréal has a vibrant nightlife scene, with everything from trendy bars and clubs to intimate jazz venues. 🎶

Montréal is a city that will captivate you with its charm, energy, and cultural richness. Come experience the magic for yourself! ✨

Québec City

This enchanting city, perched on a cliff overlooking the St. Lawrence River, is a UNESCO World Heritage Site and the only walled city north of Mexico. Imagine cobblestone streets lined with 17th-century buildings, the aroma of freshly baked croissants wafting from charming cafés, and the sound of French spoken with a delightful accent. This is Québec City, a place where history, culture, and romance intertwine to create an unforgettable experience.

A Journey Through Time:

Québec City is a living museum, a place where the past is present at every turn. I wandered through the Upper Town (Haute-Ville), exploring the Citadelle, a star-shaped fortress that offers panoramic views of the city and the river. I strolled along the Dufferin Terrace, a wooden boardwalk overlooking the St. Lawrence, and imagined the countless people who have walked this same path throughout history. And I marveled at the Château Frontenac, a majestic hotel that looks like a castle straight out of a storybook.

European Charm with a Canadian Twist: 🍁
Québec City exudes a European charm that is unique in North America. The French influence is evident in the architecture, the language, and the cuisine. But Québec City is also distinctly Canadian, with its friendly people, its love of the outdoors, and its embrace of winter. I enjoyed a delicious meal of poutine (fries, cheese curds, and gravy) at a sidewalk café, then bundled up for a walk through the snow-covered streets, admiring the twinkling lights and festive decorations. ❄

A City of Festivals: 🎉
Québec City loves to celebrate! Throughout the year, the city hosts a variety of festivals, from the Winter Carnival, a winter wonderland of snow sculptures and ice slides, to the Festival d'été de Québec, a massive music festival that draws international artists. I was lucky enough to experience the Québec City Summer Festival, where I danced the night away to live music in the streets, surrounded by a joyful crowd. 🎵

Beyond the Walls: ■
While the historic walled city is the main attraction, Québec City also offers plenty to see and do beyond its fortifications. I took a ferry across the St. Lawrence River to Lévis, a charming town with stunning views of the city skyline. I explored the Plains of Abraham, a historic battlefield that is now a beautiful park, and I visited the Montmorency Falls, a waterfall that is even taller than Niagara Falls! ●

Tips for Exploring Québec City:

- Brush up on your French: While English is spoken in tourist areas, knowing a few basic French phrases will enhance your experience and show respect for the local culture. "Bonjour!" and "Merci!" are a great start. ●
- Dress for the weather: Québec City experiences all four seasons, so be prepared for hot summers, cold winters, and everything in between. Pack layers and don't forget your winter gear if you're visiting during the colder months. ❄

- Explore on foot: The historic walled city is best explored on foot. Wear comfortable shoes and be prepared to climb some hills. 🔨
- Take a food tour: Québec City has a rich culinary tradition. A food tour is a great way to sample local specialties and learn about the city's food culture. ⚫
- Embrace the festive spirit: Québec City is a city that loves to celebrate. If you're visiting during a festival, be sure to join in the fun! 🎉

Québec City is a city that will transport you to another time and place.Come experience the magic for yourself! ✨

The Laurentian Mountains

This vast mountain range, just north of Montréal, is a true four-season playground, offering something for everyone, no matter the time of year.

Winter Wonderland: ❄️⛷️
When winter blankets the Laurentians in a pristine layer of snow, it transforms into a magical wonderland. I spent a week in Mont-Tremblant, a world-renowned ski resort, and it was pure bliss! I carved my way down the slopes, feeling the wind in my hair and the sun on my face. 🏂 Afterwards, I warmed up with a cup of hot chocolate by a crackling fireplace in a cozy chalet. 🔥 Even if you're not a skier, there's plenty to do in the winter, from snowshoeing and cross-country skiing to ice skating and dog sledding. 🐕

Spring Awakening: 🍀🌷
As the snow melts and the days get longer, the Laurentians awaken with a burst of colour and life.Wildflowers bloom in meadows, birdsong fills the air, and the forests come alive with the sound of rushing waterfalls. 💧 I hiked through the Mont-Tremblant National Park, breathing in the fresh air and marveling at the beauty of nature's rebirth. Spring is also a great time for maple syrup season! I visited a sugar shack, where I learned how maple sap is collected and transformed into delicious syrup. And of course, I indulged in a traditional pancake breakfast with maple syrup – yum! 🥞

Summer Adventures: 🛶
Summer in the Laurentians is all about outdoor adventures. I went kayaking on Lac Tremblant, surrounded by the towering mountains and lush forests. 🛶

I hiked to the summit of Mont Tremblant, enjoying panoramic views of the surrounding landscape. And I spent a day at a water park, cooling off with thrilling slides and refreshing dips in the pool. ◆ Whether you're seeking adrenaline-pumping activities or relaxing days by the lake, the Laurentians has something for you.

Autumn Splendor: ◆◆

Autumn in the Laurentians is a feast for the senses. The forests erupt in a blaze of colour, with fiery reds, oranges, and yellows painting the landscape. I took a scenic drive along the Chemin du Roy, a historic route that winds its way through the Laurentians, stopping to admire the breathtaking views and capture the beauty with my camera. ◼ Autumn is also a great time for apple picking! I visited an orchard, where I picked my own apples and enjoyed fresh apple cider and warm apple pie. ◆▶

Charming Villages & Cozy Stays: ◆

The Laurentians is dotted with charming villages, each with its own unique character. I explored the quaint town of Saint-Sauveur, with its art galleries, boutiques, and restaurants. I wandered through the historic streets of Val-David, known for its vibrant arts scene. And I stayed in a cozy cabin nestled in the woods, enjoying the peace and tranquility of nature. ▲

Tips for Exploring the Laurentians:

- Plan your trip according to your interests: Whether you're a skier, a hiker, a foodie, or a culture enthusiast, the Laurentians has something for you. Do your research and choose activities that suit your interests and the season.
- Embrace the outdoors: The Laurentians is a paradise for outdoor enthusiasts. Pack your hiking boots, your swimsuit, and your sense of adventure! ◣
- Explore the villages: Don't just stick to the main tourist areas. Venture off the beaten path and discover the charm of the smaller villages. ◆

- Indulge in the local cuisine: The Laurentians is known for its delicious food, from maple syrup and cheese to fresh produce and local wines. Don't miss the opportunity to sample the regional specialties. ●
- Relax and recharge: The Laurentians is a place to escape the hustle and bustle of city life and reconnect with nature. Take your time, breathe in the fresh air, and enjoy the peace and tranquility. ●

The Laurentian Mountains are a true gem, offering a diverse range of experiences throughout the year. Come discover the magic for yourself! ✦

Gaspesie Peninsula

This rugged peninsula jutting out into the Gulf of St. Lawrence is a place where the mountains meet the sea, creating a landscape of dramatic beauty and unparalleled wildlife encounters. Imagine driving along a coastal highway with breathtaking views, hiking through lush forests, and kayaking alongside whales in crystal-clear waters.

Coastal Charm:

The Gaspésie Peninsula boasts a coastline that will take your breath away. Rugged cliffs plunge into the turquoise waters of the Gulf of St. Lawrence, while charming fishing villages nestle in sheltered coves. I drove along Route 132, the main coastal highway, stopping at every scenic lookout to capture the beauty with my camera. The views were simply mesmerizing! I also took a boat tour to Percé Rock, a massive limestone formation that rises dramatically from the sea. It's a sight that you won't soon forget. ●

Wildlife Encounters:

Gaspésie is a haven for wildlife, and I was lucky enough to have some incredible encounters. I went whale watching in Forillon National Park and was thrilled to see humpback whales breaching and spouting just meters from our boat. ● I also hiked through the park, keeping my eyes peeled for black bears, moose, and white-tailed deer. And I spent an afternoon birdwatching, spotting puffins, gannets, and other seabirds nesting on the cliffs.

Outdoor Adventures: 🏔️🏍️

For outdoor enthusiasts, Gaspésie is a paradise. I hiked to the summit of Mont Albert, the highest peak in the Chic-Choc Mountains, enjoying panoramic views of the surrounding landscape. I cycled along the Route Verte, a network of bike paths that crisscross the peninsula. And I kayaked in the Baie des Chaleurs, paddling through calm waters and exploring hidden coves. 🛶

Charming Villages & Local Flavours: 🏘️🔴

Gaspésie is dotted with charming villages, each with its own unique character. I explored the historic town of Percé, with its colourful houses and lively waterfront. I visited the fishing village of Gaspé, where I learned about the region's maritime heritage.And I enjoyed the relaxed atmosphere of Carleton-sur-Mer, a popular seaside resort town. Of course, no trip to Gaspésie would be complete without sampling the local seafood. I feasted on fresh lobster, crab, and shrimp, savouring the flavours of the sea. 🦐🦀

Tips for Exploring Gaspésie:

- Plan your route: Gaspésie is a large peninsula, so it's important to plan your route in advance. Decide which areas you want to explore and how much time you want to spend in each place. 📖
- Book your accommodations in advance: Gaspésie is a popular tourist destination, especially during the summer months. Be sure to book your accommodations well in advance, especially if you're visiting during peak season. 🎒
- Pack for all types of weather: Gaspésie can experience all four seasons in a single day. Be prepared for sunshine, rain, and even fog. 🌦️🧳
- Learn some basic French: While English is spoken in tourist areas, knowing a few basic French phrases will enhance your experience and show respect for the local culture. "Bonjour!" and "Merci!" are a great start. ⚫

Gaspésie is a land of breathtaking scenery, abundant wildlife, and warm hospitality. Come experience the magic for yourself! ✨

CHAPTER 3

Ontario

T oronto is the most multicultural city in the world. With over 200 different languages spoken, this vibrant city is a melting pot of cultures, offering a diverse culinary scene, vibrant neighborhoods, and a cosmopolitan atmosphere.

Toronto

This vibrant city, the largest in Canada, is a whirlwind of energy, diversity, and excitement. Imagine a place where towering skyscrapers meet charming Victorian architecture, where bustling markets offer flavours from around the world, and where world-class museums and galleries stand alongside trendy boutiques and hidden laneway cafes.

Toronto is often called "the most multicultural city in the world," and for good reason! People from over 200 different countries call this city home, creating a vibrant tapestry of cultures, languages, and traditions. I wandered through Kensington Market, a bohemian neighbourhood with vintage shops, eclectic cafes, and street art murals.

I explored Chinatown, with its bustling markets and delicious dim sum restaurants. And I strolled through Little Italy, savouring the aroma of freshly baked bread and enjoying a cappuccino at a sidewalk cafe. ◼ Each neighbourhood offered a unique glimpse into a different part of the world, all within the same city.

Urban Adventures: 🚲🦅
Toronto is a city that begs to be explored. I hopped on a bike and cycled along the waterfront, enjoying the views of Lake Ontario and the city skyline. I took a ferry to the Toronto Islands, a chain of islands with beaches, parks, and amusement rides. I climbed the CN Tower, the iconic symbol of Toronto, and marveled at the panoramic views from the observation deck. And I caught a show in the Entertainment District, enjoying the vibrant theatre scene. 🦅

Hidden Gems & Local Treasures: ♦
Toronto is full of hidden gems, just waiting to be discovered. I stumbled upon Graffiti Alley, a laneway transformed into an outdoor art gallery with vibrant murals. I explored the Distillery District, a historic area with cobblestone streets, Victorian architecture, and trendy shops and restaurants. And I wandered through Evergreen Brick Works, a former industrial site that has been transformed into a vibrant community space with farmers markets, gardens, and cultural events. 🌱

Foodie Delights: ●
Toronto's food scene is as diverse as its population. I savoured delicious dumplings in Chinatown, enjoyed authentic Ethiopian food in Little Ethiopia, and indulged in a gourmet burger at a trendy gastropub. And of course, no trip to Toronto would be complete without trying poutine, the Canadian classic of fries, cheese curds, and gravy. ●

Tips for Exploring Toronto:

- Embrace the diversity: Toronto is a city where you can experience the world in one place. Explore different neighbourhoods, try new foods, and immerse yourself in the multicultural atmosphere. ●

- Get a Presto card: This reloadable card is the easiest way to pay for public transportation in Toronto. You can use it on the subway, buses, and streetcars. ▬
- Explore on foot or by bike: Toronto is a very walkable city, and there are also many bike paths. Exploring on foot or by bike is a great way to get a feel for the different neighbourhoods. 🚶
- Check out the events calendar: Toronto has a vibrant arts and culture scene, with festivals, concerts, and events happening throughout the year. Check the events calendar to see what's on during your visit. ■
- Don't be afraid to ask for directions: Torontonians are generally friendly and helpful. If you get lost, don't hesitate to ask for directions. ●

Toronto is a city that will energize and inspire you with its vibrant culture, diverse experiences, and urban adventures. Come experience the magic for yourself! ✦

Niagara Falls

This iconic waterfall, straddling the border between Canada and the United States, is a true force of nature, a mesmerizing display of raw power and beauty that leaves you speechless. Imagine standing at the brink of the falls, feeling the mist on your face and hearing the deafening roar of millions of gallons of water cascading over the precipice. This is Niagara Falls, a natural wonder that will leave you in awe. ✦

A Sensory Overload: 👣🖐

My first encounter with Niagara Falls was nothing short of overwhelming. The sheer scale of the falls is simply breathtaking. I stood on the Canadian side, gazing at the Horseshoe Falls, the largest of the three waterfalls that make up Niagara Falls. The water thundered down with incredible force, creating a cloud of mist that rose high into the air. Rainbows danced in the spray, adding a touch of magic to the scene. ✒ I could feel the ground vibrate beneath my feet, a testament to the immense power of nature.

Up Close and Personal: 🛥

To truly experience the power of Niagara Falls, you have to get up close and personal. I took a boat ride on the Maid of the Mist, which takes you right into the heart of the Horseshoe Falls. Wearing a bright yellow poncho, I felt the full force of the spray as the boat approached the falls. It was exhilarating! The roar of the water was deafening, and the mist was so thick that I could barely see.But it was an unforgettable experience, one that I will cherish forever.

Beyond the Falls: ◼

While the falls themselves are the main attraction, there's plenty more to see and do in Niagara Falls. I explored the Niagara Glen Nature Reserve, a peaceful oasis with hiking trails, waterfalls, and a unique ecosystem.I visited the Niagara Parks Butterfly Conservatory, a tropical paradise filled with thousands of colourful butterflies. 🦋 And I took a ride on the Niagara SkyWheel, a giant Ferris wheel that offers stunning views of the falls and the surrounding area. 🎡

Nighttime Magic: ✦

Niagara Falls is just as impressive at night, when the falls are illuminated with colourful lights. I watched the nightly illumination show, mesmerized by the changing colours and patterns that danced across the water.It was a truly magical experience.

Tips for Experiencing Niagara Falls:

- Visit both the Canadian and American sides: Each side offers a different perspective of the falls. The Canadian side offers panoramic views of the Horseshoe Falls, while the American side offers closer views of the American Falls and Bridal Veil Falls. ▰▰
- Take a boat ride: A boat ride on the Maid of the Mist (or the Hornblower Niagara Cruises on the Canadian side) is a must-do experience. It's the best way to feel the full force of the falls. 🛥
- Explore the Niagara Parks: The Niagara Parks system offers a variety of attractions, from gardens and historical sites to hiking trails and amusement parks. ◼

- Don't forget your camera: Niagara Falls is a photographer's dream. Be sure to capture the beauty of the falls from every angle.
- Dress for the weather: The mist from the falls can make it feel cooler than it actually is. Be sure to dress in layers and bring a waterproof jacket.

Niagara Falls is a natural wonder that will leave you breathless. Come experience the magic for yourself! ✦

Ottawa

This elegant city, nestled on the banks of the Ottawa River, is the capital of Canada and a place where history, culture, and nature intertwine. Imagine strolling along canals lined with Victorian architecture, exploring world-class museums and galleries, and witnessing the Changing of the Guard ceremony on Parliament Hill.

A Capital with Character:
Ottawa is a city that wears its history with pride. As the capital of Canada, it's home to Parliament Hill, the seat of the Canadian government. I watched the Changing of the Guard ceremony, a colourful spectacle with red-coated guards and a marching band. It was a thrilling experience! I also toured the Parliament buildings, admiring the Gothic Revival architecture and learning about Canada's political system.

Museums & Galleries Galore:
Ottawa is a haven for museum and art lovers. I spent hours exploring the Canadian Museum of History, learning about Canada's rich and diverse past. I wandered through the National Gallery of Canada, admiring masterpieces by Canadian and international artists. And I visited the Canadian War Museum, a sobering but important reminder of the sacrifices made for our freedom.

Canal City:
Ottawa is often called the "Canal City" because of the Rideau Canal, a UNESCO World Heritage Site that winds its way through the heart of the city. In the summer, I rented a kayak and paddled along the canal, enjoying the views of the city and the lush greenery. In the winter, the canal transforms into the world's largest naturally frozen skating rink! I laced up my skates and glided along the ice, feeling like a kid again.

Beyond the Downtown Core: ■

While the downtown core is packed with attractions, Ottawa also offers plenty to see and do beyond the city centre. I explored the ByWard Market, a historic market with vendors selling fresh produce, local crafts, and delicious food. I visited Gatineau Park, just across the river in Quebec, and hiked through the forests, enjoying the peace and tranquility of nature. And I took a day trip to the charming town of Merrickville, known for its historic buildings and artisan shops. ▲

Foodie Finds: ●

Ottawa's food scene is a delightful mix of Canadian classics and international flavours. I enjoyed a delicious beavertail (a fried dough pastry with sweet toppings) at the ByWard Market. I savoured poutine (fries, cheese curds, and gravy) at a local pub. And I indulged in a gourmet meal at a farm-to-table restaurant. ■

Tips for Exploring Ottawa:

- Visit during Tulip Season: In the spring, Ottawa hosts the Canadian Tulip Festival, a colourful celebration with millions of tulips blooming throughout the city. ❀
- Explore the ByWard Market: This historic market is a great place to find souvenirs, sample local food, and soak up the atmosphere. 🛍
- Take a walk or bike ride along the Rideau Canal: The canal offers stunning views of the city and is a great way to get some exercise. 🚲
- Visit Parliament Hill: Don't miss the opportunity to see the Changing of the Guard ceremony and tour the Parliament buildings. 🏛
- Learn about Canada's history: Ottawa is home to many museums and historical sites that tell the story of Canada's past.

Ottawa is a city that will charm you with its history, culture, and natural beauty. Come experience the magic for yourself! ✦

Algonquin Provincial Park

This vast wilderness, a heritage of forests, lakes, and rivers, is a true escape from the hustle and bustle of everyday life. Imagine paddling a canoe across a crystal-clear lake, listening to the call of loons echoing through the trees, and falling asleep under a canopy of stars. ✦

Paddling Through Paradise: 🛶
Algonquin Park is a paddler's paradise, with over 2,000 kilometers of canoe routes and countless lakes and rivers to explore. I rented a canoe and set off on a multi-day adventure, paddling through pristine waterways, portaging over rugged trails, and setting up camp on secluded islands. ■ The feeling of freedom and solitude was incredible. I dipped my paddle into the water, feeling the rhythm of the strokes and the gentle sway of the canoe. The only sounds were the calls of birds, the rustling of leaves, and the gentle lapping of water against the shore. 🦃

Camping Under the Stars: ⛺✦
There's nothing quite like camping in Algonquin Park. I pitched my tent on a secluded campsite, surrounded by towering pines and the sounds of nature. As night fell, I built a campfire, roasting marshmallows and gazing at the stars. The Milky Way stretched across the sky like a shimmering river of light. It was a magical experience, one that reminded me of the vastness of the universe and the beauty of our planet.■

Wildlife Encounters: 🐻🫎
Algonquin Park is home to a diverse array of wildlife. I kept my eyes peeled for moose, deer, and black bears as I paddled and hiked through the park. I was lucky enough to spot a moose grazing in a marsh, its antlers silhouetted against the setting sun. It was a breathtaking sight, a reminder of the wildness and beauty that still exists in our world.

Hiking Trails & Scenic Views:

Algonquin Park offers a variety of hiking trails, from easy strolls to challenging backcountry treks. I hiked the Spruce Bog Boardwalk Trail, a fascinating journey through a unique ecosystem. I also climbed the Centennial Ridges Trail, rewarded with panoramic views of the park's rolling hills and sparkling lakes.

Tips for Exploring Algonquin Park:

- Plan your trip: Algonquin Park is vast and offers a variety of activities. Decide what you want to do and how much time you want to spend in the park. You can choose from day trips, overnight camping trips, or multi-day backcountry adventures.
- Obtain permits: You'll need a permit for camping and for accessing certain areas of the park. Be sure to obtain your permits in advance, especially during peak season.
- Pack for all types of weather: Algonquin Park can experience all four seasons in a single day. Be prepared for sunshine, rain, and even snow, depending on the time of year.
- Respect wildlife: Algonquin Park is home to many wild animals. Keep a safe distance from wildlife, store your food properly, and make noise while hiking to avoid surprising bears.
- Leave no trace: Help protect the beauty of Algonquin Park by following Leave No Trace principles. Pack out all your trash, stay on marked trails, and minimize your impact on the environment.

Algonquin Park is a place where you can escape the everyday and immerse yourself in the beauty of the Canadian wilderness. Come experience the magic for yourself!

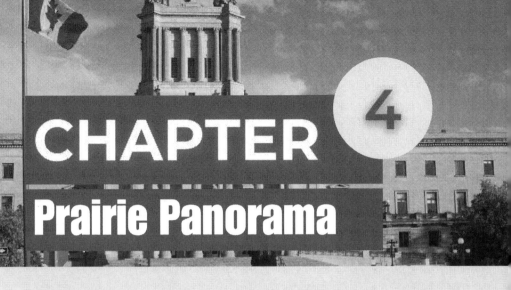

CHAPTER 4

Prairie Panorama

Alberta is home to the Canadian Badlands, a unique and dramatic landscape. Explore hoodoos, canyons, and fossil beds, and discover the prehistoric secrets of this fascinating region.

Manitoba

This province, nestled in the heart of Canada, is a land of contrasts, where vast prairies meet Arctic tundra, where bustling cities coexist with charming small towns, and where polar bears roam freely in their natural habitat.

Imagine witnessing the northern lights dancing across the sky, kayaking alongside beluga whales in the Churchill River, and exploring historic forts and vibrant cultural centers. This is Manitoba, a hidden gem that offers a unique blend of adventure, culture, and natural beauty. ✦ Churchill, a town on the shores of Hudson Bay, is known as the "Polar Bear Capital of the World." I embarked on a tundra buggy adventure, a specially designed vehicle that allows you to safely observe polar bears in their natural habitat. It was an incredible experience!

I saw these majestic creatures up close, watching them play, hunt, and interact with their cubs. It was a humbling experience, a reminder of the power and fragility of nature.

Prairie Landscapes & Golden Fields:

Manitoba is also known for its vast prairies, a seemingly endless expanse of golden fields stretching to the horizon. I drove along the Trans-Canada Highway, mesmerized by the rolling hills, the big sky, and the sense of endless space. I stopped at small towns along the way, each with its own unique character and charm. I visited farmers' markets, where I sampled local produce and homemade goods. And I enjoyed the peace and quiet of the prairies, a welcome respite from the hustle and bustle of city life.

Winnipeg:

Winnipeg, the capital of Manitoba, is a vibrant city with a rich history and a thriving arts and culture scene. I explored The Forks, a historic meeting place where the Red and Assiniboine rivers converge. I visited the Canadian Museum for Human Rights, a powerful and moving museum that explores human rights issues from around the world. And I caught a show at the Royal Manitoba Theatre Centre, enjoying the city's vibrant performing arts scene.

Festival Fun & Outdoor Adventures:

Manitoba hosts a variety of festivals throughout the year, celebrating everything from music and dance to food and culture. I experienced the Festival du Voyageur, a winter festival that celebrates the fur trade history of the province. I also enjoyed the Winnipeg Folk Festival, a multi-day music festival with a diverse lineup of artists. And for outdoor enthusiasts, Manitoba offers plenty of opportunities for adventure, from hiking and biking to kayaking and canoeing.

Tips for Exploring Manitoba:

- Plan your trip according to your interests: Whether you're interested in wildlife viewing, cultural experiences, or outdoor adventures, Manitoba has something for you. Do your research and choose activities that suit your interests.
- Visit Churchill during polar bear season: The best time to see polar bears in Churchill is from October to November, when they gather on the shores of Hudson Bay waiting for the ice to freeze.
- Explore Winnipeg's diverse neighbourhoods: Winnipeg is a city of neighbourhoods, each with its own unique character and charm. Take some time to explore different areas, from the historic Exchange District to the trendy Osborne Village.
- Embrace the outdoors: Manitoba offers a wealth of outdoor activities, from hiking and biking to fishing and kayaking. Get out and explore the natural beauty of the province.

Manitoba is a land of contrasts, where you can experience the thrill of seeing polar bears in the wild, the tranquility of the prairies, and the vibrancy of a multicultural city. Come experience the magic for yourself!

Saskatchewan

This province, often called "Canada's breadbasket," is a land of wide-open skies, endless prairies, and fascinating history. Imagine driving through fields of golden wheat that stretch as far as the eye can see, hiking through badlands where dinosaurs once roamed, and experiencing the vibrant culture of First Nations communities. This is Saskatchewan, a place where you can connect with nature, uncover ancient secrets, and discover the heart of the Canadian prairies. ✦

Golden Waves of Grain: 🌾

Saskatchewan is known as the "breadbasket of Canada" for a reason. Its fertile plains produce a vast amount of wheat, making it one of the world's leading grain producers. I drove through the countryside, mesmerized by the endless fields of golden wheat swaying in the breeze. It was like a sea of gold, stretching to the horizon. I visited a working farm, where I learned about the process of growing and harvesting wheat, and I even got to try my hand at driving a combine! 🚜

Dinosaur Discoveries: 🦖

Saskatchewan is also a hotbed for dinosaur discoveries! I visited the T.rex Discovery Centre in Eastend, where I saw Scotty, the largest Tyrannosaurus rex skeleton ever found in Canada. It was awe-inspiring! I also explored the Eastend Historical Museum, which houses a collection of fossils and exhibits on the region's paleontological history. I learned about the fascinating creatures that once roamed these lands, and I even got to participate in a fossil dig! ⛏

Vibrant Cities & Charming Towns: 🏙🏠

Saskatchewan is home to vibrant cities and charming towns, each with its own unique character. I explored Saskatoon, a city known for its lively arts scene and beautiful riverfront. I visited Regina, the capital city, and learned about Saskatchewan's political history at the Legislative Building. And I wandered through the charming town of Moose Jaw, known for its tunnels, its mineral spa, and its friendly locals.

First Nations Culture & Heritage:

Saskatchewan has a rich Indigenous history, and I had the opportunity to learn about the culture and traditions of the First Nations people. I visited Wanuskewin Heritage Park, a cultural center that showcases the history and traditions of the Northern Plains Indigenous people. I participated in a traditional drumming circle, learned about medicinal plants, and listened to stories told by elders. It was a powerful and moving experience, a reminder of the deep connection between the land and its people.

Outdoor Adventures & Natural Wonders: ⬛

Saskatchewan offers a wealth of outdoor adventures. I hiked through Grasslands National Park, a vast expanse of prairie grasslands where bison roam freely. I kayaked on Lake Diefenbaker, enjoying the peace and quiet of the water. And I visited Cypress Hills Interprovincial Park, a unique ecosystem with forests, grasslands, and stunning views. 🌲

Tips for Exploring Saskatchewan:

- Embrace the wide-open spaces: Saskatchewan is a province of vast distances and big skies. Rent a car and explore the countryside, stopping at small towns and enjoying the scenery along the way.
- Visit during the summer months: The best time to visit Saskatchewan is during the summer (June-August), when the weather is warm and sunny. However, the province also offers unique experiences in other seasons, such as the northern lights in the winter.
- Learn about First Nations culture: Saskatchewan has a rich Indigenous history. Visit a cultural center, attend a powwow, or participate in a traditional ceremony to learn about the culture and traditions of the First Nations people.
- Explore the cities and towns: Saskatchewan has a variety of cities and towns, each with its own unique character. Spend some time exploring Saskatoon, Regina, Moose Jaw, and other communities to get a feel for the province's diverse culture.
- Enjoy the local hospitality: Saskatchewanians are known for their friendly and welcoming nature. Don't be afraid to strike up a conversation with the locals and learn about their way of life.

Saskatchewan is a land of golden fields, dinosaur discoveries, and vibrant culture. Come experience the magic for yourself!

Alberta

This province, a land of rugged beauty and vibrant spirit, is where the majestic Canadian Rockies meet the rolling foothills, where cowboy culture thrives, and where outdoor adventures abound. Imagine hiking through turquoise lakes and snow-capped peaks, witnessing the Calgary Stampede, a rodeo spectacle like no other, and exploring charming mountain towns with a Wild West flair.

Rocky Mountain High: 🔺

The Canadian Rockies, a UNESCO World Heritage Site, are the crown jewel of Alberta. I stood in awe of their towering peaks, their snow-capped summits glistening in the sunlight. I hiked through Banff National Park, a wonderland of turquoise lakes, alpine meadows, and glaciers. I took a gondola ride up Sulphur Mountain, enjoying panoramic views of the Bow Valley. And I soaked in the Banff Upper Hot Springs, surrounded by the stunning mountain scenery. ■

Cowboy Country: 🤠

Alberta is also cowboy country, a place where the spirit of the Wild West lives on. I visited Calgary, home of the Calgary Stampede, a world-famous rodeo and exhibition. I watched cowboys compete in thrilling events like bull riding and barrel racing. I learned about the history of the Stampede and the importance of cowboy culture in Alberta. And I even tried my hand at line dancing! 🤠

Dinosaur Discoveries: 🦖

Did you know that Alberta is a hotbed for dinosaur discoveries? I visited the Royal Tyrrell Museum of Palaeontology in Drumheller, where I saw a vast collection of dinosaur fossils, including the impressive Albertosaurus.

I learned about the prehistoric creatures that once roamed these lands, and I even got to participate in a fossil dig!

Charming Towns & City Life:
Alberta is home to charming towns and vibrant cities, each with its own unique character. I explored Banff, a picturesque mountain town with a vibrant arts scene and a relaxed atmosphere. I visited Canmore, a charming town nestled in the Bow Valley, known for its outdoor activities and stunning scenery. And I experienced the energy of Edmonton, the capital city, with its museums, galleries, and festivals.

Outdoor Adventures:
Alberta is an outdoor enthusiast's dream come true. I went hiking, biking, and kayaking in the Rocky Mountains. I went whitewater rafting on the Kicking Horse River, an adrenaline-pumping experience! I even tried skiing in the winter, enjoying the powdery slopes and stunning views.

Tips for Exploring Alberta:

- Plan your trip according to your interests: Whether you're interested in exploring the mountains, experiencing cowboy culture, or discovering dinosaur history, Alberta has something for you. Do your research and choose activities that suit your interests.
- Visit during the summer months for optimal weather: The best time to visit Alberta is during the summer (June-August), when the weather is warm and sunny. However, the province also offers unique experiences in other seasons, such as skiing in the winter and seeing the northern lights.
- Embrace the cowboy spirit: Alberta is a province with a strong cowboy culture. Attend a rodeo, visit a ranch, or learn about the history of the Wild West.
- Enjoy the natural beauty: Alberta is home to some of the most stunning scenery in the world. Take some time to appreciate the mountains, lakes, and forests.
- Alberta is a land of breathtaking scenery, vibrant culture, and endless adventure. Come experience the magic for yourself!

CHAPTER 5

Pacific Coast Paradise

Vancouver is consistently ranked as one of the most livable cities in the world. With its stunning natural beauty, vibrant cultural scene, and diverse neighborhoods, it's easy to see why.

Vancouver

This vibrant city, nestled between the mountains and the sea, is a place where urban sophistication meets natural beauty. Imagine strolling through lush parks, exploring bustling markets, and gazing at snow-capped peaks, all within the same day.

Vancouver is a city that embraces its natural surroundings. Everywhere I looked, I saw lush greenery, from the towering trees in Stanley Park to the vibrant flowerbeds in Queen Elizabeth Park. I strolled along the seawall, a scenic pathway that winds its way along the waterfront, enjoying the fresh air and the stunning views of the ocean and mountains. I visited Granville Island Market, a bustling marketplace with vendors selling fresh produce, seafood, and local crafts.

And I explored Gastown, Vancouver's oldest neighbourhood, with its cobblestone streets, Victorian architecture, and trendy shops and restaurants.

Mountain Majesty: ▲

Vancouver is blessed with a stunning backdrop: the Coast Mountains. I took a gondola ride up Grouse Mountain, enjoying panoramic views of the city, the ocean, and the surrounding peaks. I hiked the Grouse Grind, a challenging but rewarding trail that leads to the summit. And I even saw a grizzly bear at the Grouse Mountain Refuge for Endangered Wildlife! 🐻

Cultural Fusion: ●

Vancouver is a city of diverse cultures, with a rich history of immigration. I explored Chinatown, one of the largest Chinatowns in North America, with its bustling markets, delicious dim sum restaurants, and traditional Chinese medicine shops. I visited the Museum of Anthropology at UBC, which houses a fascinating collection of First Nations art and artifacts. And I enjoyed the vibrant nightlife in the Granville Entertainment District, with its diverse mix of bars, clubs, and live music venues. 🎵

Outdoor Adventures: 🚵 kayaking

Vancouver is a haven for outdoor enthusiasts. I rented a bike and cycled through Stanley Park, enjoying the forest trails and the ocean views. I went kayaking in False Creek, paddling past the city skyline and enjoying the peaceful waters. And I took a ferry to Bowen Island, a charming island with hiking trails, beaches, and a relaxed atmosphere.

Tips for Exploring Vancouver:

- Embrace the outdoors: Vancouver is a city that encourages an active lifestyle. Go for a hike, rent a bike, or explore the waterways by kayak or paddleboard. ■
- Visit Stanley Park: This 1,000-acre park is a must-see, with its forest trails, beaches, and stunning views of the city and the ocean. 🌲

- Explore Granville Island Market: This bustling marketplace is a feast for the senses, with vendors selling fresh produce, seafood, and local crafts. 🍎
- Take a day trip to the mountains or the islands: Vancouver is surrounded by natural beauty. Take a day trip to Grouse Mountain, Bowen Island, or Whistler for a change of scenery. ▲
- Enjoy the diverse culinary scene: Vancouver has a vibrant food scene, with influences from around the world. Try some dim sum in Chinatown, enjoy fresh seafood at Granville Island, or indulge in a gourmet meal at a trendy restaurant. 🍷

Vancouver is a city that will captivate you with its natural beauty, urban sophistication, and vibrant culture. Come experience the magic for yourself! ✨

Vancouver Island

Vancouver Island! Oh, how I adore this place! It's an island paradise where rugged coastlines meet lush rainforests, where charming towns nestle amidst towering trees, and where whales breach in the sparkling waters. Imagine hiking through ancient forests, kayaking alongside orcas, and exploring historic villages with a laid-back island vibe.

This is Vancouver Island, a place where you can escape the ordinary and embrace the beauty of nature and the tranquility of island life. ✦

Whale Watching Wonderland:

Vancouver Island is one of the best places in the world for whale watching! I embarked on a whale watching tour from Victoria, the island's charming capital city. As we sailed through the Salish Sea, I felt the excitement building. And then, there they were! A pod of orcas, their black and white bodies sleek and powerful, swimming alongside our boat. I watched in awe as they breached, their massive bodies leaping out of the water, and spyhopped, their heads popping up to get a better look at us. It was a truly unforgettable experience. ●

Island Adventures: 🥾🚴

Vancouver Island is a haven for outdoor enthusiasts. I hiked through the ancient forests of Pacific Rim National Park Reserve, marveling at the towering trees and the lush undergrowth. I cycled along the Galloping Goose Trail, a scenic pathway that winds its way through forests, meadows, and charming towns. And I kayaked in the Broken Group Islands, a collection of over 100 islands and islets with hidden coves, sandy beaches, and abundant wildlife.

Charming Towns & Island Culture: 🏘️

Vancouver Island is dotted with charming towns and villages, each with its own unique character. I explored Victoria, the capital city, with its historic buildings, beautiful gardens, and vibrant harbour. I visited Tofino, a laid-back surf town on the west coast, known for its stunning beaches and laid-back vibe. And I wandered through the quaint town of Chemainus, famous for its outdoor murals depicting the history of the area.

Island Life: 👥🦀

Vancouver Island is a place where people embrace a slower pace of life. I visited a local farmers' market, where I sampled fresh produce, homemade jams, and artisan cheeses. I enjoyed a seafood feast at a waterfront restaurant, savouring the fresh catch of the day. And I even tried my hand at crabbing, pulling up traps filled with delicious Dungeness crabs! 🦀

Tips for Exploring Vancouver Island:

- Plan your route: Vancouver Island is a large island, so it's important to plan your route in advance. Decide which areas you want to explore and how much time you want to spend in each place. 📖
- Book your accommodations in advance: Vancouver Island is a popular tourist destination, especially during the summer months. Be sure to book your accommodations well in advance, especially if you're visiting during peak season. 🧳
- Pack for all types of weather: Vancouver Island can experience a variety of weather conditions, from sunshine and warm temperatures to rain and fog. Be prepared for anything! 🌧️
- Explore by car or ferry: The best way to explore Vancouver Island is by car. You can also take ferries to different parts of the island, including the Gulf Islands and the Sunshine Coast. ⛴️

Vancouver Island is a place where you can escape the ordinary and embrace the beauty of nature and the tranquility of island life. Come experience the magic for yourself! ✨

Whistler

This vibrant mountain resort town, nestled in the Coast Mountains of British Columbia, is a haven for outdoor enthusiasts and adventure seekers. Imagine carving down pristine slopes, soaring through the air on a zipline, and soaking in breathtaking alpine scenery. This is Whistler, a place where you can push your limits, embrace the thrill of adventure, and experience the magic of the mountains.

Powder Paradise: ❄

Whistler Blackcomb is renowned as one of the best ski resorts in the world, and it's easy to see why! I strapped on my skis and hit the slopes, feeling the rush of adrenaline as I carved down the mountain. The snow was powdery perfection, and the views were simply breathtaking. With over 8,100 acres of terrain, there's something for everyone, from beginner slopes to challenging black diamond runs. I even took a lesson from a friendly instructor, who helped me improve my technique and conquer new challenges. 🎿

Beyond the Slopes: 🎿

Even if you're not a skier or snowboarder, Whistler has plenty to offer. I went snowshoeing through the forests, enjoying the peace and quiet of the winter wonderland. I took a thrilling ride on the PEAK 2 PEAK Gondola, the longest and highest lift in the world, soaring above the mountains and enjoying panoramic views. And I warmed up with a delicious hot chocolate at a cozy mountaintop cafe. ☕

Summertime Fun:

Whistler is a year-round destination, and the summer months offer a whole new set of adventures. I hiked through alpine meadows, surrounded by wildflowers and breathtaking scenery. I mountain biked down thrilling trails, feeling the wind in my hair and the adrenaline pumping. And I went ziplining through the forest canopy, soaring through the air like a bird. 🏔

Village Vibe: 🏘

Whistler Village is a charming pedestrian village with a lively atmosphere. I strolled through the streets, browsing the shops, enjoying the outdoor patios, and soaking up the mountain town vibe. I even caught a free concert in the village square, enjoying live music under the stars. 🎶

Tips for Exploring Whistler:

- Plan your trip according to your interests: Whether you're a skier, a hiker, a mountain biker, or simply someone who enjoys stunning scenery, Whistler has something for you. Do your research and choose activities that suit your interests and the season.
- Purchase a Whistler Blackcomb lift ticket: If you're planning to ski or snowboard, be sure to purchase a lift ticket in advance, especially during peak season. You can also purchase a multi-day pass for the best value. 🎿
- Explore the village: Whistler Village is a charming pedestrian village with shops, restaurants, and activities for all ages. Take some time to wander around and soak up the atmosphere. 🏘
- Embrace the adventure: Whistler is a place where you can push your limits and try new things. Don't be afraid to step outside your comfort zone and embrace the thrill of adventure. ✨

Whistler is a world-class destination for outdoor enthusiasts and adventure seekers. Come experience the magic for yourself! ✨

The Okanagan Valley

This sun-drenched valley, nestled in the heart of British Columbia, is a place where rolling hills meet sparkling lakes, where vineyards bask in the warm sunshine, and where a relaxed, lakeside lifestyle beckons. Imagine sipping award-winning wines on a patio overlooking a vineyard, kayaking on a crystal-clear lake, and exploring charming towns with a laid-back vibe.

Wine Wonderland:

The Okanagan Valley is Canada's premier wine region, boasting over 180 wineries producing a diverse range of award-winning wines. I embarked on a wine tour, visiting vineyards nestled on rolling hillsides, sampling delicious reds, whites, and rosés. I learned about the unique terroir of the Okanagan, the soil and climate that give the wines their distinctive character. And I enjoyed gourmet meals paired with local wines at picturesque wineries.

Lakeside Living:

The Okanagan Valley is also home to a string of stunning lakes, perfect for swimming, boating, and paddling. I spent a day kayaking on Okanagan Lake, the largest lake in the valley, enjoying the warm sunshine and the breathtaking views of the surrounding mountains. I also visited Kalamalka Lake, known for its vibrant turquoise waters, and Skaha Lake, a popular spot for windsurfing and kitesurfing.

Charming Towns & Fruitful Delights: 🎒🍇

The Okanagan Valley is dotted with charming towns and villages, each with its own unique character. I explored Kelowna, the largest city in the valley, with its vibrant cultural scene, bustling waterfront, and diverse culinary offerings. I visited Penticton, a charming town nestled between two lakes, known for its beaches, wineries, and fruit orchards. And I wandered through the quaint town of Osoyoos, the warmest place in Canada, enjoying the desert landscape and the laid-back atmosphere.

Outdoor Adventures: 🥾🚵

The Okanagan Valley is a haven for outdoor enthusiasts. I hiked through scenic trails in Myra-Bellevue Provincial Park, enjoying panoramic views of the valley and the surrounding mountains. I cycled along the Kettle Valley Rail Trail, a former railway line that has been converted into a scenic pathway. And I went fruit picking in one of the many orchards that dot the valley, enjoying fresh peaches, cherries, and apples straight from the tree. 🍎🍒

Tips for Exploring the Okanagan Valley:

- Plan your trip according to your interests: Whether you're a wine enthusiast, a water sports lover, or an outdoor adventurer, the Okanagan Valley has something for you. Do your research and choose activities that suit your interests.
- Visit during the summer months for optimal weather: The best time to visit the Okanagan Valley is during the summer (June-August), when the weather is warm and sunny, perfect for enjoying the lakes and wineries.
- Explore the wineries: The Okanagan Valley is home to over 180 wineries. Take a wine tour, visit a few wineries on your own, or attend a wine festival to experience the best of the region's wine scene. 🍷
- Enjoy the lakes: The Okanagan Valley is blessed with stunning lakes. Go for a swim, rent a kayak or paddleboard, or take a boat tour to enjoy the scenery. 🚤

- Embrace the relaxed lifestyle: The Okanagan Valley is a place to slow down and enjoy the simple things. Take your time, explore the charming towns, and soak up the natural beauty. ●

The Okanagan Valley is a place where you can indulge in the finer things in life, soak up the natural beauty, and escape to a world of tranquility and charm. Come experience the magic for yourself! ✦

CHAPTER 6

Northern Territories

T he Yukon is home to Mount Logan, the highest mountain in Canada. This majestic peak, reaching 5,959 meters, is a testament to the raw beauty and power of the Canadian wilderness.

Yukon

This territory, in Canada's far north, is a land of raw beauty, untamed wilderness, and captivating history. Imagine paddling down a river where gold nuggets were once plucked from the banks, hiking through landscapes where towering mountains meet vast boreal forests, and witnessing the ethereal glow of the Northern Lights dancing across the night sky

The Yukon's history is forever intertwined with the Klondike Gold Rush, a period of feverish excitement that drew thousands of fortune seekers to the territory in the late 19th century.

I visited Dawson City, a town that sprang up during the gold rush and still retains its Wild West charm. I walked along the wooden boardwalks, imagining the prospectors who once walked these same streets. I toured historic buildings, like the Palace Grand Theatre and Diamond Tooth Gerties Gambling Hall, and learned about the fascinating stories of the gold rush era. I even tried my hand at gold panning in the Klondike River, hoping to strike it rich! (No luck this time, but the experience was golden! ●)

Wilderness Wonders: ▪

The Yukon is a vast and untamed wilderness, a place where nature reigns supreme. I hiked through Kluane National Park and Reserve, a UNESCO World Heritage Site, marveling at the towering peaks of the St. Elias Mountains and the vast glaciers that carve their way through the landscape. I paddled down the Yukon River, following in the footsteps of the gold rush stampeders, enjoying the peace and tranquility of the flowing water. And I camped under the stars, surrounded by the sounds of nature, feeling a deep connection to the wilderness. ▪

Northern Lights Spectacle: ✦

The Yukon is one of the best places in the world to witness the aurora borealis, or Northern Lights. I bundled up in warm clothes and ventured out into the night, gazing up at the sky in anticipation. And then, it happened! The sky erupted in a dazzling display of colour, with green, pink, and purple lights dancing across the heavens. It was a magical experience, one that I will never forget.

Wildlife Encounters: ▪▪

The Yukon is home to a diverse array of wildlife. I saw a grizzly bear fishing for salmon in a river, its massive paws scooping up the fish with ease. I watched a bald eagle soar through the sky, its wingspan stretching wide. And I heard the haunting howl of a wolf echoing through the forest. The Yukon is a place where you can truly experience the wildness of nature.

Tips for Exploring the Yukon:

- Plan your trip according to your interests: Whether you're interested in history, wildlife, or outdoor adventures, the Yukon has something for you. Do your research and choose activities that suit your interests.

- Visit during the summer for warmer weather: The best time to visit the Yukon for outdoor activities is during the summer (June-August), when the weather is mild and the days are long. However, the winter months offer the opportunity to see the Northern Lights and experience the unique beauty of a winter wonderland. ❄

- Embrace the remoteness: The Yukon is a vast and sparsely populated territory. Be prepared for long distances, limited services, and the need to be self-sufficient.

- Respect the wilderness: The Yukon is a wild and unforgiving place. Be prepared for encounters with wildlife, unpredictable weather, and challenging terrain. Always follow safety guidelines and respect the environment.

The Yukon is a land of adventure, history, and untamed beauty. Come experience the magic for yourself! ✦

Northwest Territories

This vast and rugged territory, stretching across Canada's Arctic region, is a land of breathtaking landscapes, incredible wildlife, and vibrant Indigenous cultures. Imagine gazing at the mesmerizing dance of the Northern Lights, paddling through pristine lakes surrounded by towering mountains, and learning about the traditions of the Dene, Inuit, and Métis people. This is the Northwest Territories, a place where you can experience the raw beauty of the Arctic, witness natural wonders, and connect with the resilient spirit of the North. ✨

Aurora Borealis Magic: ✨

The Northwest Territories is one of the best places in the world to witness the aurora borealis, or Northern Lights. I ventured out of Yellowknife, the capital city, on a clear winter night, far from any city lights. As I looked up at the sky, I was awestruck by the mesmerizing display of colours dancing across the heavens. Shimmering curtains of green, pink, and purple rippled and swirled, creating a celestial ballet that took my breath away. It was a truly magical experience, one that I will never forget.

Diamond Capital of North America: ◆

The Northwest Territories is also known as the "Diamond Capital of North America," thanks to its rich diamond deposits. I visited a diamond mine and learned about the fascinating process of extracting these precious gems from the earth. I even got to hold a rough diamond in my hand, marveling at its sparkle and beauty.

Land of the Midnight Sun:

During the summer months, the Northwest Territories experiences the "midnight sun," a phenomenon where the sun never sets. I witnessed this incredible sight, where the sun hovered above the horizon, casting a golden glow over the landscape even at midnight. It was a surreal and unforgettable experience.

Arctic Adventures: ▬

The Northwest Territories offers a wealth of outdoor adventures. I paddled a canoe through Great Slave Lake, the deepest lake in North America, surrounded by stunning scenery and abundant wildlife. I hiked through Nahanni National Park Reserve, a UNESCO World Heritage Site, marveling at the towering canyons, cascading waterfalls, and pristine rivers. And I went fishing for Arctic char, a delicious fish that thrives in the cold northern waters. 🎣

Indigenous Cultures & Traditions:

The Northwest Territories is home to diverse Indigenous communities, each with its own rich culture and traditions. I visited the Yellowknives Dene First Nation, where I learned about their history, their connection to the land, and their traditional way of life. I participated in a drumming circle, listened to stories told by elders, and learned about the importance of preserving their cultural heritage.

Tips for Exploring the Northwest Territories:

- Plan your trip according to your interests: Whether you're interested in seeing the Northern Lights, exploring the wilderness, or learning about Indigenous cultures, the Northwest Territories has something for you. Do your research and choose activities that suit your interests.
- Visit during the shoulder seasons for optimal weather: The shoulder seasons (spring and fall) offer pleasant weather and fewer crowds. However, the winter months offer the opportunity to see the Northern Lights, and the summer months offer the midnight sun and warmer temperatures.
- Embrace the remoteness: The Northwest Territories is a vast and sparsely populated territory. Be prepared for long distances, limited services, and the need to be self-sufficient.
- Respect the environment and wildlife: The Northwest Territories is a pristine environment. Follow Leave No Trace principles, respect wildlife, and be mindful of your impact on the land.
- Learn about the Indigenous cultures: The Northwest Territories is home to diverse Indigenous communities. Visit cultural centers, attend events, and engage respectfully with local people to learn about their rich cultures and traditions.

The Northwest Territories is a land of breathtaking beauty, incredible wildlife, and vibrant Indigenous cultures. Come experience the magic for yourself! ✦

Nunavut

This vast territory, spanning Canada's eastern Arctic, is a land of stark beauty, ancient traditions, and incredible wildlife. Imagine kayaking amongst icebergs under the midnight sun, witnessing the majestic polar bear in its natural habitat, and learning about the rich culture of the Inuit, the original inhabitants of this land.

This is Nunavut, a place where you can experience the raw power of the Arctic, connect with a resilient culture, and witness some of the most incredible wildlife on Earth. ✦

Land of the Inuit:

Nunavut is home to the Inuit, a people who have thrived in the Arctic for thousands of years. I visited Iqaluit, the capital city, and was warmly welcomed by the Inuit community. I learned about their history, their traditions, and their deep connection to the land. I visited the Nunatta Sunakkutaangit Museum, which showcases Inuit art, artifacts, and stories. And I attended a traditional throat singing performance, mesmerized by the haunting sounds and rhythmic movements.

Arctic Wildlife Encounters: 🐻‍❄️🐋

Nunavut is a wildlife lover's paradise. I embarked on an Arctic safari, venturing out onto the tundra in search of polar bears, muskoxen, and caribou. I witnessed a polar bear hunting seals on the ice, its powerful body moving with grace and agility. I saw a herd of muskoxen grazing on the tundra, their thick coats protecting them from the cold. And I watched caribou migrating across the vast landscape, their antlers silhouetted against the horizon.

Land of Ice and Snow: ❄●

Nunavut is a land of ice and snow, where glaciers carve through mountains, and icebergs drift along the coast. I took a boat tour through the ice-choked waters of the Arctic Ocean, marveling at the towering icebergs, their shapes and colours constantly changing in the light. I hiked across the tundra, feeling the crunch of snow beneath my feet and breathing in the crisp Arctic air. And I witnessed the incredible beauty of the Northern Lights dancing across the night sky. ✦

Unique Cultural Experiences:

Nunavut offers a variety of unique cultural experiences. I visited a traditional Inuit camp, where I learned about their way of life, their hunting and fishing techniques, and their close relationship with the land. I tried traditional Inuit food, like Arctic char and bannock, savoring the unique flavours of the North. And I learned a few words of Inuktitut, the Inuit language, attempting to connect with the local culture on a deeper level.

Tips for Exploring Nunavut:

- Plan your trip carefully: Nunavut is a remote and challenging environment. Do your research, book tours and accommodations in advance, and be prepared for unpredictable weather and limited services.
- Visit during the shoulder seasons for milder weather: The shoulder seasons (spring and fall) offer milder weather and fewer crowds. However, the winter months offer the opportunity to see the Northern Lights, and the summer months offer the midnight sun and warmer temperatures.
- Pack for all types of weather: Nunavut can experience extreme weather conditions, from frigid temperatures and blizzards in the winter to surprisingly warm temperatures and mosquitos in the summer. Be prepared for anything!

- Respect the environment and wildlife: Nunavut is a pristine environment. Follow Leave No Trace principles, respect wildlife, and be mindful of your impact on the land.
- Learn about the Inuit culture: Nunavut is home to a rich and vibrant Inuit culture. Visit cultural centers, attend events, and engage respectfully with local people to learn about their traditions and way of life.

Nunavut is a land of stark beauty, ancient traditions, and incredible wildlife. Come experience the magic for yourself! ✦

CHAPTER 7

A Feast for the Senses

Canada is the world's largest producer of maple syrup. Indulge in this sweet treat, a true Canadian icon, and discover the traditional process of tapping maple trees and boiling the sap into syrup. Canada has a thriving craft beer scene.

From Coast to Coast

This vast and diverse country is a culinary adventure waiting to happen. From the fresh seafood of the Atlantic coast to the hearty game meats of the north, each region boasts its own unique flavors and local specialties. Join me on a mouthwatering journey from coast to coast, as we explore the delicious diversity of Canadian cuisine. ✨

Atlantic Canada: 🦞🦀

- My culinary journey began in Atlantic Canada, where the ocean's bounty takes center stage.

- Newfoundland and Labrador: I savored cod tongues, a local delicacy that surprised me with its delicate flavor. I also indulged in Jiggs dinner, a hearty Sunday meal with salt beef, potatoes, and cabbage.
- Nova Scotia: I feasted on fresh lobster, enjoying lobster rolls, lobster bisque, and even lobster poutine! I also sampled Digby scallops, known for their sweet and delicate flavor.
- Prince Edward Island: Of course, I had to try the famous PEI mussels, known for their plumpness and briny sweetness. And I couldn't resist a classic lobster supper, complete with all the fixings.
- New Brunswick: I discovered the unique flavor of fiddleheads, a springtime delicacy that tastes like a cross between asparagus and spinach. And I enjoyed poutine râpée, a traditional Acadian dish made with grated potatoes and pork.

Quebec:
Quebec's cuisine is a delightful blend of French influences and local ingredients.

- Montreal: I indulged in flaky croissants and pain au chocolat at charming patisseries. And I savored poutine, the iconic dish of fries, cheese curds, and gravy.
- Quebec City: I enjoyed classic French dishes like tourtière, a savory meat pie, and tarte au sucre, a sweet sugar pie.
- The Laurentians: I visited a sugar shack and enjoyed a traditional pancake breakfast with maple syrup, a true Canadian treat. ●

Ontario: ●
Ontario's diverse population is reflected in its vibrant culinary scene.

- Toronto: I explored the city's multicultural neighborhoods, enjoying authentic dim sum in Chinatown, flavorful Ethiopian stews in Little Ethiopia, and delicious jerk chicken in Little Jamaica.
- Niagara Falls: I sampled local wines at Niagara-on-the-Lake, a charming town known for its vineyards. 🍷
- Ottawa: I tried a beavertail, a fried dough pastry with sweet toppings, a popular treat in the capital city.

The Prairies: 🦌

The Prairie provinces offer hearty dishes and locally sourced ingredients.

- Manitoba: I savored Winnipeg goldeye, a smoked fish unique to the region. And I enjoyed pierogies, a Ukrainian dumpling dish that has become a local favorite.
- Saskatchewan: I tried Saskatoon berries, a sweet and juicy berry that is used in pies, jams, and other treats. And I enjoyed a hearty plate of bison stew, a local specialty.
- Alberta: I feasted on Alberta beef, known for its quality and flavor. And I indulged in a delicious butter chicken, a popular dish with Indian influences.

British Columbia: ●

British Columbia's cuisine is a fusion of fresh seafood, local produce, and Asian flavors.

- Vancouver: I enjoyed fresh sushi and sashimi at one of the city's many Japanese restaurants. And I savored West Coast salmon, grilled to perfection.
- Vancouver Island: I indulged in a seafood feast, enjoying fresh Dungeness crab, spot prawns, and oysters.
- The Okanagan Valley: I sampled local wines and enjoyed farm-to-table cuisine, savoring fresh fruits and vegetables from the valley's orchards and farms.

The North: 🦌

The Northern Territories offer unique culinary experiences, with wild game and traditional Indigenous dishes.

- Yukon: I tried Arctic char, a delicious fish that thrives in the cold northern waters. And I sampled bannock, a traditional Indigenous bread.
- Northwest Territories: I enjoyed caribou stew, a hearty dish made with local game meat. And I tried muktuk, a traditional Inuit dish made with whale skin and blubber.

- Nunavut: I savored Arctic char prepared in a variety of ways, from smoked to grilled to raw. And I learned about the importance of traditional food sources like seal and caribou to the Inuit people.

Canada's culinary scene is a reflection of its diverse landscape and multicultural heritage. From coast to coast, there's a delicious adventure waiting to be discovered. So, come hungry and explore the regional flavors and local specialties that make Canadian cuisine so unique and unforgettable! ✦●❤

Beyond Poutine

While poutine is undeniably a Canadian icon (and trust me, it's delicious!), there's a whole world of flavors waiting to be discovered in the Great White North. Join me on a mouthwatering adventure as we explore some must-try Canadian dishes that go beyond the classic fries, cheese curds, and gravy. ✦

From Coast to Coast:
Canada's diverse regions offer a smorgasbord of unique culinary creations. Here are a few of my favorites:

Atlantic Canada:

- Newfoundland and Labrador: I braved the cod tongues (yes, really!) and was pleasantly surprised by their delicate, flaky texture. Don't knock it 'til you try it! ●
- Nova Scotia: Digby scallops, seared to perfection and bursting with sweet, briny flavor, were an absolute delight. ●
- Prince Edward Island: The classic lobster supper is a must-try, piled high with fresh lobster, mussels, clams, and potatoes. 🦞
- New Brunswick: Fiddleheads, a unique springtime delicacy, were a revelation! They have a slightly nutty flavor and a tender-crisp texture. 🌱

Quebec:

- Montreal: Beyond poutine, I discovered the joy of Montreal smoked meat, piled high on rye bread with mustard. It's a carnivore's dream!
- Quebec City: Tourtière, a savory meat pie, warmed my soul on a chilly evening. It's a comforting and flavorful dish, perfect for sharing. ▶

Ontario:

- Toronto: The city's multiculturalism shines through in its diverse food scene. I sampled delicious jerk chicken in Little Jamaica, flavorful butter chicken in Little India, and authentic dim sum in Chinatown. ●
- Ottawa: BeaverTails, a fried dough pastry topped with cinnamon sugar, chocolate, or other sweet treats, were a delightful indulgence. ●

The Prairies:

- Manitoba: Winnipeg goldeye, a smoked fish with a unique flavor, is a local delicacy. It's often served with crackers and cream cheese.
- Saskatchewan: Saskatoon berry pie is a must-try! The berries have a sweet and slightly tart flavor, perfect for a summer dessert. ▶
- Alberta: Alberta beef is legendary for its quality and flavor. I enjoyed a juicy steak cooked to perfection, a true taste of the Canadian West. ●

British Columbia:

- Vancouver: West Coast salmon, grilled or smoked, is a culinary highlight. The fish is incredibly fresh and flavorful. ●
- Vancouver Island: Nanaimo bars, a no-bake dessert with a chocolate, custard, and coconut base, are a decadent treat. ◆

The North:

- Yukon: Bannock, a traditional Indigenous bread, is a versatile staple. It can be enjoyed plain or with various toppings.
- Northwest Territories: Arctic char, a delicate fish with a slightly sweet flavor, is a culinary gem. It can be prepared in a variety of ways, from grilled to smoked. ◀
- Nunavut: Muktuk, a traditional Inuit dish made with whale skin and blubber, is a unique and adventurous culinary experience.

Farm-to-Table Experiences and Culinary Tours

From meeting passionate farmers to indulging in gourmet meals crafted with locally sourced ingredients, these experiences connect you with the land, the people, and the culinary traditions that make Canada so special. ✦

In British Columbia's Okanagan Valley, I embarked on a culinary adventure that tantalized my taste buds. I visited a family-owned orchard, where I plucked juicy peaches and crisp apples straight from the tree. 🍎🍎 The taste of sun-ripened fruit, warm from the orchard's embrace, was pure heaven! Later, I dined at a farm-to-table restaurant, where the menu showcased the valley's bounty. Each dish was a masterpiece, crafted with fresh, local ingredients and bursting with flavor. I savored roasted vegetables still warm from the garden, tender lamb raised on a nearby farm, and a decadent dessert made with local berries and honey. ●

Prince Edward Island Delights: 🦞●

Prince Edward Island, with its fertile red soil and abundance of fresh seafood, is a farm-to-table paradise. I joined a culinary tour that took me to a local potato farm, where I learned about the island's famous spuds and even helped harvest some from the field! ● Later, I enjoyed a lobster feast at a waterfront restaurant, where the lobster was so fresh it practically jumped off the plate! 🦞 The combination of fresh-caught seafood and locally grown produce was a true taste of PEI.

Ontario's Culinary Trails: 🍷

Ontario offers a variety of culinary trails that showcase the province's diverse agricultural landscape. I explored the Niagara Wine Route, stopping at charming wineries to sample award-winning wines and learn about the winemaking process. 🍷 I also ventured along the Apple Pie Trail, indulging in homemade pies made with fresh-picked apples from local orchards. ● Each stop on the trail offered a unique taste of Ontario's culinary heritage.

Quebec's Country Charm: 🍁

In Quebec, I escaped the city and ventured into the countryside, where I discovered charming farms and local producers. I visited a maple syrup farm, where I learned about the traditional process of tapping maple trees and boiling the sap into sweet, golden syrup. I even got to taste the syrup fresh from the evaporator – it was divine! Later, I enjoyed a delicious meal at a farm-to-table restaurant, where the menu featured local cheeses, fresh produce, and, of course, plenty of maple syrup. ●

Tips for Farm-to-Table Experiences:

- Do your research: Look for farm-to-table restaurants, culinary tours, and farmers' markets in the regions you'll be visiting. Many farms also offer tours and tastings.
- Embrace the seasonality: Farm-to-table cuisine is all about using fresh, seasonal ingredients. Be open to trying new things and savoring the flavors of each season.
- Support local businesses: By choosing farm-to-table experiences, you're supporting local farmers, producers, and businesses, contributing to the local economy and sustainable practices.
- Savor the experience: Take your time, enjoy the flavors, and appreciate the connection between the land, the people, and the food you're enjoying.

Farm-to-table experiences offer a unique and delicious way to connect with Canada's culinary landscape. So, grab your appetite and embark on a culinary adventure that will nourish your body and soul! ✦

Canada's Craft Beer and Wine Scene

Canada's craft beverage scene is booming, with innovative breweries and wineries popping up from coast to coast. Get ready to tantalize your taste buds with unique brews and delightful vintages, all while experiencing the passion and creativity of Canadian brewers and vintners. ✦

Canada's craft beer scene has exploded in recent years, with microbreweries popping up in every province and territory. I embarked on a beer-tasting adventure, sampling a diverse range of brews, from hoppy IPAs and rich stouts to fruity sours and crisp lagers.

- British Columbia: In Vancouver, I explored the vibrant brewery scene, hopping from Granville Island Brewing to Steamworks Brewpub, enjoying the laid-back atmosphere and the innovative brews. 🍺
- Alberta: In Calgary, I visited Big Rock Brewery, a pioneer in the Canadian craft beer movement, and sampled their classic brews alongside new experimental creations.
- Ontario: Toronto's craft beer scene is thriving, with breweries like Bellwoods Brewery and Great Lakes Brewery offering unique and flavorful beers. I even took a brewery tour, learning about the brewing process and meeting the passionate people behind the pints.
- Quebec: Montreal's microbreweries are known for their creativity and bold flavors. I sampled delicious brews at Dieu du Ciel!, a brewery with a cult following, and enjoyed the lively atmosphere of pub crawls and beer festivals. 🍺
- Atlantic Canada: Even in the Maritimes, craft breweries are making a splash. I visited Garrison Brewing in Halifax and Propeller Brewing in Nova Scotia, enjoying local brews with a maritime twist.

Wine Regions with a View: 🍷🍇

Canada's wine scene is also flourishing, with diverse wine regions offering unique terroir and award-winning vintages.

- British Columbia: The Okanagan Valley is a wine lover's paradise, with vineyards nestled amongst rolling hills and overlooking sparkling lakes. I sipped on crisp whites, bold reds, and fruity rosés, enjoying the stunning scenery and the warm hospitality of the wineries. 🍷
- Ontario: The Niagara Peninsula is another renowned wine region, producing world-class wines, particularly icewine, a sweet dessert wine made from grapes frozen on the vine. I toured vineyards, sampled delicious wines, and learned about the unique challenges and rewards of growing grapes in this region. 🍇
- Nova Scotia: Even in the cooler climate of Nova Scotia, wineries are producing unique and flavorful wines. I visited Gaspereau Vineyards, enjoying their Tidal Bay wines, a crisp and refreshing white wine unique to Nova Scotia.

Tips for Exploring Canada's Craft Beverage Scene:

- Check out local breweries and wineries: Do your research and find out which breweries and wineries are located in the regions you'll be visiting. Many offer tours, tastings, and special events.
- Attend a beer or wine festival: These festivals are a great way to sample a variety of brews and vintages, meet the brewers and vintners, and enjoy live music and entertainment. 🍺🎶
- Ask for recommendations: Locals are often the best source of information on the best breweries and wineries in their area. Don't be afraid to ask for recommendations from bartenders, servers, and shop owners.

Canada's craft beer and wine scene is a testament to the country's creativity, innovation, and passion for quality. So, raise a glass and toast to the delicious discoveries that await! 🍺🍷

CONCLUSION

Final Thoughts & Encouragement

As I close this travel guide, my heart overflows with the memories of my Canadian adventures. From the rugged coastlines of the Atlantic to the majestic peaks of the Rockies, from the vibrant cities to the charming towns, Canada has captured my soul. This country, a mosaic of cultures and landscapes, offers something for everyone, whether you seek adventure, tranquility, or simply the joy of discovering new horizons. But Canada is more than just its breathtaking scenery and diverse experiences. It's the warmth of the people, the spirit of generosity, and the sense of community that truly make it special. I've been welcomed with open arms wherever I've gone, sharing laughter, stories, and a genuine connection with Canadians from all walks of life.

So, pack your bags, embrace your adventurous spirit, and prepare to be amazed by the wonders of Canada. This is a land that will stay with you long after you've returned home, a place that will beckon you back to explore its hidden corners and uncover its endless charms.

Until next time, Canada!

APPENDICES

Essential Phrases in French

While English is widely spoken across Canada, knowing a few essential French phrases can greatly enhance your experience, especially in Quebec, where French is the official language. Not only will it help you navigate everyday situations, but it also shows respect for the local culture and can lead to more meaningful interactions with the people you meet. ● I remember feeling a bit lost when I first arrived in Montreal. I knew a little French from high school, but I was definitely rusty! However, I quickly discovered that even a few basic phrases, like "bonjour" (hello) and "merci" (thank you), went a long way. People appreciated the effort, and it often led to friendly conversations and helpful tips. ●

So, whether you're ordering a croissant in a Parisian-style cafe or asking for directions to a hidden gem, these essential French phrases will help you navigate your Canadian adventure with confidence and connect with the local culture on a deeper level. ✦

Greetings and Essentials:
- Bonjour! (bohn-zhoor) - Hello! This is the most common greeting, used throughout the day.
- Bonsoir! (bohn-swar) - Good evening! Use this after around 6 pm.
- Au revoir! (oh ruh-vwah) - Goodbye!
- Merci! (mehr-see) - Thank you!

- S'il vous plaît (seel voo pleh) - Please.
- Excusez-moi (eks-kyoo-zay mwah) - Excuse me.
- Oui (wee) - Yes.
- Non (noh) - No.
- Je ne comprends pas. (zhuh nuh kohm-prahn pah) - I don't understand.
- Parlez-vous anglais? (par-lay voo ahn-glay?) - Do you speak English?

Dining and Shopping:

- Je voudrais... (zhuh voo-dray) - I would like...
- Un café, s'il vous plaît. (uhn ka-fay, seel voo pleh) - A coffee, please.
- L'addition, s'il vous plaît. (la-dee-syohn, seel voo pleh) - The bill, please.
- C'est combien? (seh kohm-bee-en?) - How much is it?
- Où sont les toilettes? (oo sohn lay twah-let?) - Where are the restrooms?

Getting Around:

- Où est...? (oo eh...?) - Where is...?
- la gare? (la gar) - the train station?
- l'aéroport? (la-ay-roh-pohr) - the airport?
- le centre-ville? (luh sohn-truh-veel) - the city center?
- un taxi? (uhn tak-see) - a taxi?

Helpful Phrases:

- Je suis perdu(e). (zhuh swee pehr-doo/pehr-doo) - I am lost. (masculine/feminine)
- Pouvez-vous m'aider? (poo-vay voo meh-day?) - Can you help me?
- Je ne sais pas. (zhuh nuh say pah) - I don't know.
- C'est magnifique! (seh ma-nyee-feek!) - It's magnificent!
- Merci beaucoup! (mehr-see boh-koo) - Thank you very much!

Currency Converter and Tipping Guide

Navigating a new currency and tipping customs can sometimes feel like a puzzle, but fear not, fellow adventurers! ● This guide will equip you with the knowledge you need to handle your money matters like a pro and ensure smooth and happy transactions throughout your Canadian journey. ✦

Canadian Currency: ●
Canada uses the Canadian dollar (CAD), which is divided into 100 cents. You'll find coins and banknotes in various denominations. Here's a fun fact: Canadians affectionately call the $1 coin a "loonie" because it features a loon (a type of bird) on one side, and the $2 coin a "toonie" because, well, it's two loonies! ●

Currency Exchange: 💱

- Before You Go: It's often a good idea to exchange some of your currency for Canadian dollars before your trip, especially if you're arriving late at night or in a smaller town where exchange services might be limited.
- At the Airport: Currency exchange kiosks are readily available at airports, but they might have less favorable exchange rates.
- Banks and ATMs: Banks and ATMs offer convenient ways to exchange currency and withdraw cash. Keep in mind that ATMs might charge transaction fees.
- Credit Cards: Credit cards are widely accepted in Canada, but it's always a good idea to have some cash on hand, especially for smaller purchases or in more rural areas.

Tipping:
Tipping is customary in Canada for services in restaurants, bars, taxis, and hotels. It's a way to show your appreciation for good service and acknowledge the hard work of those in the service industry. Here's a general guideline:

- Restaurants: 15-20% of the pre-tax bill is standard for good service. You can adjust the amount based on the quality of service.
- Bars: $1-2 per drink or 15-20% of the total bill.
- Taxis: 10-15% of the fare.
- Hotels: $2-5 per night for housekeeping, $1-2 per bag for bellhops.

Tipping Tips: ●

- Cash or Card: Tipping in cash is common, but many establishments also allow you to add a tip to your credit card payment.
- Exceptional Service: Feel free to tip more generously for exceptional service that goes above and beyond.
- Poor Service: While it's rare, if you receive poor service, you can choose to tip less or not at all. However, it's always a good idea to speak to the manager first to address any concerns.
- Be Mindful of Local Customs: Tipping customs can vary slightly from province to province. When in doubt, it's always a good idea to observe what locals do or ask for advice from your hotel concierge.

Budgeting for Your Trip: 💰

- Estimate Your Expenses: Before your trip, research the average costs of accommodation, food, transportation, and activities in the regions you'll be visiting. This will help you create a realistic budget.
- Track Your Spending: Keep track of your expenses during your trip to ensure you're staying within your budget. You can use a budgeting app, a notebook, or simply keep your receipts.
- Be Prepared for Unexpected Costs: It's always a good idea to have a buffer in your budget for unexpected expenses, such as souvenirs, medical costs, or travel delays.

Money-Saving Tips: 🎋

- Look for Deals and Discounts: Take advantage of travel deals, discounts for students or seniors, and free activities like hiking and exploring parks.

Transportation Resources

Canada is a vast and exciting country, and you'll need reliable transportation to explore all its hidden gems. From soaring through the skies to cruising along scenic highways, this guide will help you navigate your transportation options like a pro and ensure smooth travels throughout your Canadian adventure. ✈

Air Travel: ✈

- Major Airlines: Canada has several major airlines, including Air Canada, WestJet, and Porter Airlines, offering domestic and international flights. I've flown with Air Canada numerous times, and I've always been impressed with their service and comfortable flights. ●

- Regional Airlines: For reaching smaller communities and remote areas, regional airlines like Central Mountain Air and First Air are your go-to options.

- Booking Flights: I recommend booking your flights in advance, especially during peak season, to secure the best deals and availability. You can use online travel agencies, airline websites, or contact a travel agent for assistance.

- Airport Transfers: Most airports offer various transportation options for getting to your destination, including taxis, ride-sharing services (like Uber and Lyft), airport shuttles, and public transportation.

Train Travel: 🚃

- VIA Rail: VIA Rail is Canada's national passenger railway service, offering scenic routes that connect major cities and towns across the country. I took a VIA Rail train from Toronto to Vancouver, and it was an incredible experience! The views were breathtaking, and the onboard service was excellent. I highly recommend train travel for a relaxing and scenic way to see Canada. ■

- Rocky Mountaineer: For a luxurious train journey through the Canadian Rockies, consider the Rocky Mountaineer. This train offers panoramic views, gourmet meals, and personalized service. It's definitely a splurge, but it's an unforgettable experience. ✦

Car Rentals: 🚗

- Rental Companies: Major car rental companies like Hertz, Avis, and Budget operate in Canada. I usually compare prices and options online before choosing a rental company.
- Driver's License: You'll need a valid driver's license from your home country or an International Driving Permit to rent a car in Canada.
- Insurance: Make sure you have adequate insurance coverage for your rental car.
- Road Rules: Familiarize yourself with Canadian road rules and regulations, which might differ from those in your home country.
- Navigation: Consider renting a GPS device or using a navigation app on your smartphone to help you navigate Canadian roads.

Public Transportation: 🚌

- Cities: Most Canadian cities have efficient public transportation systems, including buses, subways, and streetcars. I found the public transportation in Toronto and Vancouver to be very convenient and affordable. You can purchase tickets or passes at stations, on board, or online.
- Smaller Towns: Smaller towns might have limited public transportation options, so it's a good idea to check schedules and routes in advance.

Other Transportation Options: 🚤🏍

- Ferries: Ferries are a common mode of transportation in coastal regions and for traveling between islands. I took a ferry from Vancouver to Vancouver Island, enjoying the scenic views of the ocean and the surrounding islands.

- Taxis and Ride-Sharing: Taxis and ride-sharing services are readily available in most cities and towns. I often use ride-sharing services like Uber and Lyft because they're convenient and usually more affordable than taxis.
- Cycling: Many cities have bike-sharing programs and dedicated bike lanes, making cycling a fun and healthy way to explore. I rented a bike in Montreal and enjoyed cycling along the Lachine Canal, enjoying the scenery and the fresh air. 🚴

Important Notes:

- Distances: Canada is a vast country, so be prepared for long distances between destinations. Plan your travel time accordingly.
- Weather Conditions: Weather conditions can vary greatly across Canada, especially in the winter. Be prepared for snow, ice, and other challenging conditions.
- Accessibility: If you have accessibility needs, be sure to research transportation options in advance and choose accessible services.

With a little planning and the right resources, you can navigate Canada's transportation network with ease and enjoy every moment of your journey.

Accommodation Directory

Finding the perfect place to rest your head after a day of exploring is essential for a truly enjoyable trip. Whether you're seeking luxurious city hotels, cozy mountain cabins, or unique wilderness retreats, Canada offers a diverse range of accommodations to suit every taste and budget. Here are a few of my personal favorites, complete with insider tips and essential information to help you plan your stay. ✦

City Chic:

- **Fairmont Le Château Frontenac, Quebec City:** 🏨 This iconic castle-like hotel, perched on a cliff overlooking the St. Lawrence River, is a landmark in itself. I splurged on a stay here, and it was worth every penny! The rooms are elegant, the service is impeccable, and the views are simply breathtaking. (Price: $$$$; Amenities: Spa, indoor pool, fine dining; Contact: +1 (418) 692-3861; Address: 1 Rue des Carrières, Québec City, QC G1R 4P5)

- **The Hazelton Hotel, Toronto:** ✦ This luxurious hotel in the heart of Yorkville, Toronto's upscale neighborhood, offers a sophisticated and stylish retreat. I loved the rooftop pool and bar, the perfect place to unwind after a day of exploring the city. (Price: $$$$; Amenities: Spa, rooftop pool, fine dining; Contact: +1 (416) 963-6300; Address: 118 Yorkville Ave, Toronto, ON M5R 1C2)

- **OPUS Hotel, Vancouver:** 🍪 This trendy boutique hotel in Yaletown, Vancouver's trendy district, is known for its modern design and vibrant atmosphere. I enjoyed the rooftop patio with its stunning city views and the cozy library with its curated collection of books. (Price: $$$; Amenities: Fitness center, rooftop patio, bar; Contact: +1 (604) 642-6787; Address: 322 Davie St, Vancouver, BC V6B 5Z6)

Mountain Majesty:

- **Fairmont Banff Springs, Banff:** ⛰ This grand hotel, nestled in the heart of Banff National Park, is a true mountain icon. I felt like royalty staying here, surrounded by breathtaking scenery and enjoying world-class amenities. (Price: $$$$; Amenities: Spa, golf course, multiple dining options; Contact: +1 (403) 762-2211; Address: 405 Spray Ave, Banff, AB T1L 1J4)

- **Nimmo Bay Wilderness Resort, Great Bear Rainforest:** 🌲 For a truly unique and unforgettable experience, I recommend Nimmo Bay. This remote wilderness resort, accessible only by floatplane, offers luxurious accommodations and incredible wildlife viewing opportunities. I saw grizzly bears, whales, and eagles during my stay! (Price: $$$$$; Amenities: Spa, guided tours, gourmet meals; Contact: +1 (250) 949-8032; Address: Nimmo Bay, BC V0P 1P0)

- **Storm Mountain Lodge, Banff National Park:** 🏔 This historic lodge, built in the 1920s, offers a cozy and rustic retreat in the heart of the Canadian Rockies. I loved the crackling fireplaces, the comfortable cabins, and the peaceful atmosphere. (Price: $$; Amenities: Restaurant, hiking trails, fire pits; Contact: +1 (403) 762-4155; Address: Banff National Park, AB T1L 1J4)

Coastal Charm:

- **Wickaninnish Inn, Tofino:** 🌊 This stunning beachfront inn on Vancouver Island offers breathtaking views of the Pacific Ocean and luxurious accommodations. I enjoyed relaxing by the fireplace in my room, listening to the waves crashing on the shore. (Price: $$$$; Amenities: Spa, oceanfront dining, surfing lessons; Contact: +1 (250) 725-3100; Address: 500 Osprey Lane, Tofino, BC V0R 2Z0)

- **Fogo Island Inn, Newfoundland and Labrador:** ⚓ This unique inn, perched on the edge of the Atlantic Ocean, offers a modern and minimalist design with stunning views of the rugged coastline. I loved the floor-to-ceiling windows in my room, which provided panoramic views of the ocean and the dramatic landscape. (Price: $$$$$; Amenities: Spa, art gallery, guided hikes; Contact: +1 (709) 658-3444; Address: 210 Main Rd, Joe Batt's Arm, NL A0G 2X0)

Unique & Quirky:

- **Free Spirit Spheres, Vancouver Island:** ● For a truly unique accommodation experience, I recommend spending a night in a Free Spirit Sphere. These spherical treehouses, suspended in the rainforest canopy, offer a peaceful and magical retreat. (Price: $$; Amenities: Basic amenities, unique experience; Contact: +1 (250) 757-9445; Address: 420 Horne Lake Rd, Qualicum Beach, BC V9K 1Z7)

- **Hotel de Glace, Quebec City:** ❄ This ice hotel, rebuilt every winter, is a truly magical experience. I spent a night in a room made entirely of ice, bundled up in warm furs and sleeping on a bed of ice. It was an adventure I'll never forget! (Price: $$$; Amenities: Ice bar, ice slide, unique experience; Contact: +1 (418) 623-2888; Address: 1860, boulevard Valcartier, Valcartier, QC G0A 4S0)

Budget-Friendly Options:

- **HI Hostels:** ♥ HI Hostels offer affordable and social accommodation options in various locations across Canada. I've stayed in several HI Hostels during my travels, and I've always enjoyed the friendly atmosphere and the opportunity to meet fellow travelers. (Price: $; Amenities: Shared dorms and private rooms, common areas, kitchens; Contact: Visit hihostels.ca for locations and contact information)

- **Bed and Breakfasts:** 🏠 Bed and breakfasts offer a cozy and personal touch, often with homemade breakfasts and local insights from your hosts. I've had some wonderful experiences staying in B&Bs, especially in smaller towns and rural areas. (Price:

- $; Amenities: Vary by location; Contact: Search online or ask for local recommendations)
- Camping: 🏕 Canada has an abundance of campgrounds, from national parks to private campgrounds. Camping is a great way to connect with nature and enjoy the outdoors. (Price: $; Amenities: Vary by location; Contact: Visit parkscanada.gc.ca or search online for private campgrounds)

Remember to book your accommodations in advance, especially during peak season! With a little planning and research, you're sure to find the perfect place to rest and recharge during your Canadian adventure.

Festival and Event Calendar

Canada comes alive with festivals and events throughout the year, celebrating everything from music and art to food and culture. These vibrant celebrations offer a fantastic opportunity to immerse yourself in local traditions, experience Canadian hospitality, and create unforgettable memories. Here's a glimpse into some of the most exciting festivals and events happening across the country, guaranteed to add a splash of colour and excitement to your Canadian adventure. ✦

Winter Wonderland: ❄

- Winterlude (Ottawa, February): I bundled up and embraced the winter fun at Winterlude, Ottawa's winter festival. I marveled at ice sculptures, skated on the Rideau Canal (the world's largest naturally frozen skating rink!), and enjoyed the festive atmosphere. ⛸
- Festival du Voyageur (Winnipeg, February): This lively festival celebrates the fur trade history of Manitoba with traditional music, food, and activities like snow sculpting and dog sledding. I even tried some delicious pea soup, a traditional Voyageur dish. ●
- Québec Winter Carnival (Quebec City, February): This iconic winter carnival is a wonderland of snow sculptures, ice slides, parades, and night-time entertainment. I felt like a kid again, sliding down the ice slides and exploring the magical ice palace. ❄

Spring Awakening: ❀

- Canadian Tulip Festival (Ottawa, May): Ottawa blooms with millions of tulips during this colourful festival, celebrating the gift of tulips from the Netherlands after World War II. I strolled through the tulip gardens, enjoying the vibrant displays and the festive atmosphere. ⚘
- Pacific Rim Whale Festival (Tofino & Ucluelet, BC, March): This festival celebrates the annual migration of gray whales to the Pacific Rim National Park Reserve. I joined a whale watching tour and was thrilled to see these majestic creatures up close. 🐋

Summer Celebrations:

- Calgary Stampede (Calgary, July): This world-famous rodeo and exhibition is a true spectacle, with thrilling rodeo events, live music, agricultural displays, and a vibrant midway. I donned my cowboy hat and embraced the Wild West spirit, watching cowboys compete in bull riding and barrel racing. 🤠
- Montreal International Jazz Festival (Montreal, June/July): This renowned jazz festival draws music lovers from around the world with its diverse lineup of artists and lively atmosphere. I enjoyed outdoor concerts, intimate club performances, and the vibrant energy of the city. 🎵
- Toronto International Film Festival (Toronto, September): This prestigious film festival showcases the best of international and Canadian cinema. I caught a few screenings, enjoyed celebrity sightings, and experienced the buzz of the city's film scene. 🎬

Autumn Delights: 🍁

- Celtic Colours International Festival (Cape Breton Island, October): This festival celebrates Cape Breton's rich Celtic heritage with music, dance, and cultural events. I attended a lively ceilidh (a traditional Gaelic social gathering with music and dancing) and was swept away by the energy and passion of the musicians. 🎻
- Oktoberfest (Kitchener-Waterloo, Ontario, October): This lively festival celebrates German heritage with traditional music, food, and beer. I donned my lederhosen and joined the festivities, enjoying oompah bands, pretzels, and, of course, plenty of beer! 🍺

Beyond the Big Festivals:

- Local Festivals: Throughout the year, smaller towns and communities host their own unique festivals, celebrating local traditions, food, and culture. I stumbled upon a charming farmers' market in Prince Edward Island, where I enjoyed live music, local crafts, and delicious homemade treats. 🍎

- Cultural Events: From powwows and Indigenous celebrations to multicultural festivals and art exhibitions, there's always something happening in Canada. I attended a powwow in Saskatchewan, where I witnessed traditional dancing, drumming, and singing, and learned about First Nations culture.

Tips for Enjoying Festivals and Events:

- Plan Ahead: Many festivals and events require tickets or reservations, especially popular ones. Book your tickets in advance to avoid disappointment.
- Check the Schedule: Festivals often have packed schedules with various activities and performances. Check the schedule in advance to plan your time and ensure you don't miss anything you're interested in.
- Embrace the Atmosphere: Festivals are a time to let loose, have fun, and embrace the festive spirit. Join in the celebrations, try new things, and connect with the local culture.
- Be Prepared for Crowds: Popular festivals can attract large crowds. Be patient, wear comfortable shoes, and stay hydrated.
- Respect Local Customs: Be mindful of local customs and traditions when attending festivals and events.

Canada's festivals and events offer a vibrant and unforgettable experience. So, mark your calendar, embrace the celebrations, and create memories that will last a lifetime! 🎉

Emergency Contact Information

While I hope your Canadian adventure is filled with nothing but joyful moments and exciting discoveries, it's always wise to be prepared for the unexpected. This guide provides essential emergency contact information and helpful tips to ensure you have a safe and worry-free journey. ✈

Important Numbers:

- Emergency Services: 911 (for police, fire, or ambulance) 🚒🚓🚑
- I remember once hiking in Banff National Park when I took a tumble and twisted my ankle. Thankfully, I had cell service and was able to call 911. The park rangers arrived quickly and helped me get back to safety. It was a reminder that even experienced adventurers can encounter unexpected situations.
- Poison Control: 1-800-268-9017 ☣
- Non-Emergency Police: (Vary by location; check local listings or ask your hotel) 🚔

Health & Safety:

- Travel Insurance: I highly recommend purchasing travel insurance before your trip. It can provide coverage for medical expenses, trip cancellations, lost luggage, and other unexpected events. I once had to cancel a trip due to a family emergency, and my travel insurance reimbursed me for the non-refundable expenses. It was a lifesaver!
- Medications: If you take any prescription medications, be sure to bring enough for your entire trip, plus a little extra in case of delays. Keep them in their original containers and carry a copy of your prescription.
- Allergies: If you have any allergies, carry an allergy alert card or wear a medical alert bracelet. Inform your travel companions and accommodation providers about your allergies.
- Vaccinations: Check with your doctor or travel clinic to ensure you have all the necessary vaccinations for your trip to Canada.

Embassy or Consulate:

Contact Information: If you're traveling from another country, it's a good idea to have the contact information for your embassy or consulate in Canada. They can provide assistance in case of emergencies, such as lost passports or legal issues.

Other Essential Information:

- Local Emergency Contacts: Keep a list of local emergency contacts, such as your hotel's front desk, your tour operator, and any local friends or family you might have.
- Important Documents: Make copies of your passport, driver's license, travel insurance policy, and other important documents.1 Keep them separate from the originals in case of loss or theft.
- Safety Tips: Be aware of your surroundings, especially in crowded areas. Keep your valuables secure and avoid walking alone at night in unfamiliar areas.
- Weather Awareness: Pay attention to weather forecasts and warnings, especially if you're planning outdoor activities. Canada can experience extreme weather conditions, so be prepared and adjust your plans accordingly.

Stay Connected:

- Cell Phone: Make sure your cell phone is unlocked and compatible with Canadian networks. Consider purchasing a local SIM card for convenient and affordable communication.
- Wi-Fi: Most hotels, cafes, and public spaces offer Wi-Fi access. You can also find free Wi-Fi hotspots in many cities and towns.
- Be Prepared, Stay Safe:

While emergencies are rare, it's always better to be prepared. By taking a few simple precautions and having essential information readily available, you can ensure a safe and enjoyable Canadian adventure.

Notre-Dame Basilica

SCAN THE QR CODE

- Open your device's camera app
- Point the camera at the QR code
- Ensure the QR code is within the frame and well-lit
- Wait for your device to recognize the QR code
- Once recognized, tap on the map and input for current location for direction and distance to the destination

Downtown Toronto

SCAN THE QR CODE

- Open your device's camera app
- Point the camera at the QR code
- Ensure the QR code is within the frame and well lit
- Wait for your device to recognize the QR code
- Once recognized, tap on the map and input for current location for direction and distance to the destination

Old Montreal

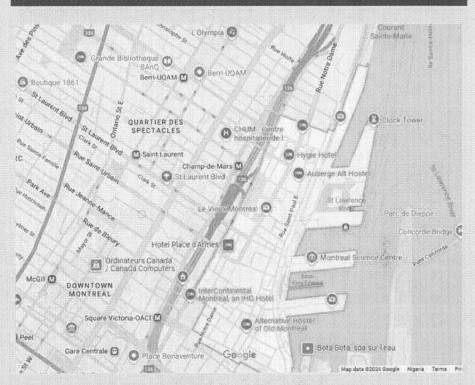

SCAN THE QR CODE

- Open your device's camera app
- Point the camera at the QR code
- Ensure the QR code is within the frame and well-lit
- Wait for your device to recognize the QR code
- Once recognized, tap on the map and input for current location for direction and distance to the destination

Quebec City

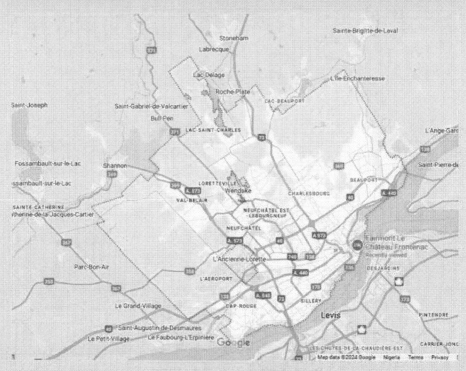

SCAN THE QR CODE

- Open your device's camera app
- Point the camera at the QR code
- Ensure the QR code is within the frame and well-lit
- Wait for your device to recognize the QR code
- Once recognized, tap on the map and input for current location for direction and distance to the destination

Downtown Vancouver

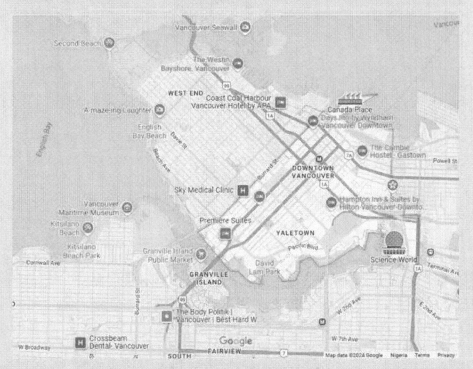

SCAN THE QR CODE

- Open your device's camera app
- Point the camera at the QR code
- Ensure the QR code is within the frame and well-lit
- Wait for your device to recognize the QR code
- Once recognized, tap on the map and input for current location for direction and distance to the destination

Downtown Ottawa

SCAN THE QR CODE

- Open your device's camera app
- Point the camera at the QR code
- Ensure the QR code is within the frame and well-lit
- Wait for your device to recognize the QR code
- Once recognized, tap on the map and input for current location for direction and distance to the destination

Niagara Falls

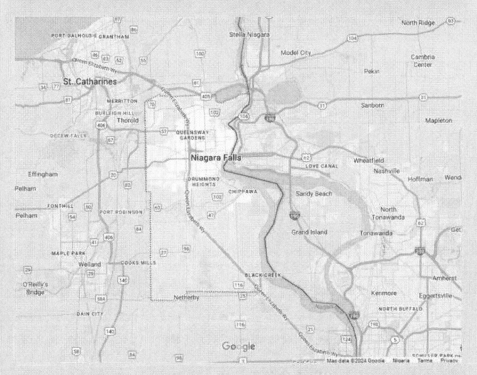

SCAN THE QR CODE

- Open your device's camera app
- Point the camera at the QR code
- Ensure the QR code is within the frame and well-lit
- Wait for your device to recognize the QR code
- Once recognized, tap on the map and input for current location for direction and distance to the destination

Whistler Blackcomb

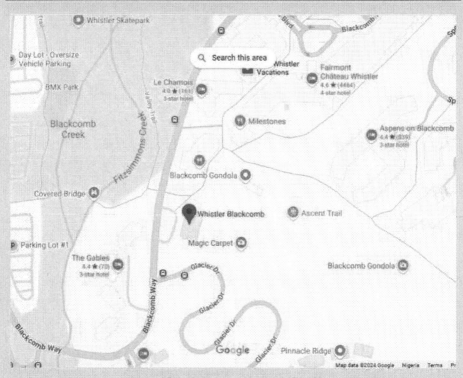

SCAN THE QR CODE

- Open your device's camera app
- Point the camera at the QR code
- Ensure the QR code is within the frame and well-lit
- Wait for your device to recognize the QR code
- Once recognized, tap on the map and input for current location for direction and distance to the destination

Stanley Park

SCAN THE QR CODE

- Open your device's camera app
- Point the camera at the QR code
- Ensure the QR code is within the frame and well-lit
- Wait for your device to recognize the QR code
- Once recognized, tap on the map and input for current location for direction and distance to the destination

Banff Gondola

Search this area

Eden

Banff Upper Hot Springs

Banff Gondola
Cableway to the top
of Sulphur Mountain

Banff Gondola

ntain
on

Banff Gondola
Upper Terminal

Google

Map data ©2024 Google   Nigeria   Terms   Priv

SCAN THE QR CODE

- Open your device's camera app
- Point the camera at the QR code
- Ensure the QR code is within the frame and well-lit
- Wait for your device to recognize the QR code
- Once recognized, tap on the map and input for current location for direction and distance to the destination

CN Tower

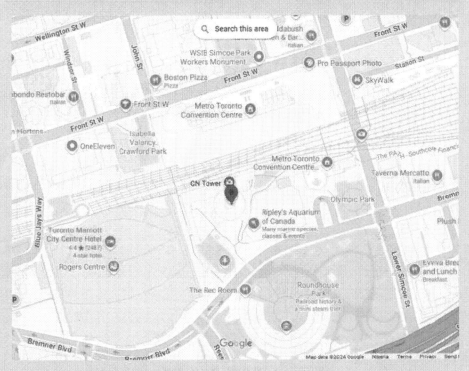

SCAN THE QR CODE

- Open your device's camera app
- Point the camera at the QR code
- Ensure the QR code is within the frame and well-lit
- Wait for your device to recognize the QR code
- Once recognized, tap on the map and input for current location for direction and distance to the destination

Moraine Lake

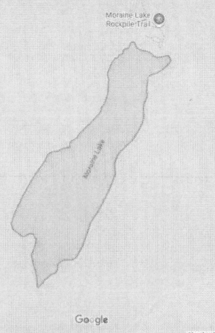

SCAN THE QR CODE

- Open your device's camera app
- Point the camera at the QR code
- Ensure the QR code is within the frame and well-lit
- Wait for your device to recognize the QR code
- Once recognized, tap on the map and input for current location for direction and distance to the destination

Churchill

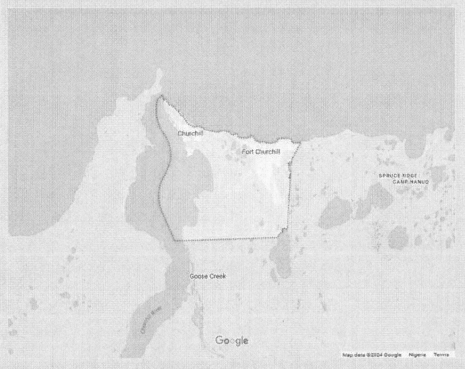

SCAN THE QR CODE

- Open your device's camera app
- Point the camera at the QR code
- Ensure the QR code is within the frame and well-lit
- Wait for your device to recognize the QR code
- Once recognized, tap on the map and input for current location for direction and distance to the destination

ENHANCE YOUR JOURNEY WITH INTERACTIVE MAPS

Scan the QR codes on the maps throughout this guide to unlock a wealth of additional information, including:

- Interactive maps: Zoom in on specific regions and attractions for detailed navigation and exploration.
- Real-time updates: Get the latest information on weather conditions, road closures, and events happening near you.
- Exclusive content: Access bonus travel tips, insider recommendations, and hidden gems not found in the book.

To scan QR codes, simply download a free QR code reader app on your smartphone. We recommend using a reliable and user-friendly app such as:

- **QR CODE SCANNER & SCANNER APP : AVAILABLE FOR BOTH IOS AND ANDROID DEVICES, THIS APP IS QUICK, EFFICIENT, AND OFFERS A SEAMLESS SCANNING EXPERIENCE.**

By utilizing these interactive maps and QR codes, you can further personalize your adventure and discover even more of what this beautiful city has to offer. Happy travels!

FROM THE AUTHOR

If this guide helped you uncover Canada's hidden treasures and create unforgettable memories, we'd love to hear about it! Your review on Amazon helps other adventurous travelers discover the magic of the beautiful country

Here's how to leave a review:

- Head to Amazon.com (or your local Amazon site).
- Search for the book by its title: "Canada Travel Guide 2025: Explore Stunning Natural Wonders and Savor Culinary Delights with Full-Color Maps."
- Once on the book's page, scroll down to the "Customer Reviews" section.
- Click on the button that says "Write a customer review".
- Give the book a star rating and share your thoughts in the text box provided.
- Hit "Submit"!

It's that easy – and your feedback is invaluable to us!

MY TRAVEL PLAN

TRAVEL ITINERARY

Date: _____

S S M T W T F

Date:

Location:

Budget:

Trip To-do List

Daily Expenses

Daily Log

6 AM

7 AM

8 AM

9 AM

10 AM

11 AM

12 PM

1 PM

2 PM

3 PM

4 PM

5 PM

6 PM

7 PM

8 PM

NOTE:

Canada Travel Guide

MY PACKING LIST

TRAVEL ITINERARY

Date: _____

S S M T W T F

THINGS TO PACK ⬤

- ◯
- ◯
- ◯
- ◯
- ◯
- ◯
- ◯
- ◯
- ◯
- ◯
- ◯
- ◯
- ◯
- ◯
- ◯
- ◯
- ◯
- ◯

ACCOMODATION

Name of Hotel

Location:

Check In Date:

Check Out Date:

Total Cost:

TRANSPORT

✈ _____

🚆 _____

🚕

NOTES

PLACES TO VISIT

TRAVEL ITINERARY

Date: _____

S S M T W T F

Place	Visitor's Review
	☆☆☆☆☆☆☆☆☆☆
	☆☆☆☆☆☆☆☆☆☆
	☆☆☆☆☆☆☆☆☆☆
	☆☆☆☆☆☆☆☆☆☆
	☆☆☆☆☆☆☆☆☆☆
	☆☆☆☆☆☆☆☆☆☆
	☆☆☆☆☆☆☆☆☆☆
	☆☆☆☆☆☆☆☆☆☆
	☆☆☆☆☆☆☆☆☆☆
	☆☆☆☆☆☆☆☆☆☆
	☆☆☆☆☆☆☆☆☆☆
	☆☆☆☆☆☆☆☆☆☆
	☆☆☆☆☆☆☆☆☆☆
	☆☆☆☆☆☆☆☆☆☆

Notes

TRAVEL JOURNAL

TRAVEL REVIEW

Today's experience

THANK YOU

FOR VISITING CANADA

ENJOY!

Made in the USA
Columbia, SC
16 March 2025

55236223R00072